BRITISH RAILWAY
STEAM
in Colour

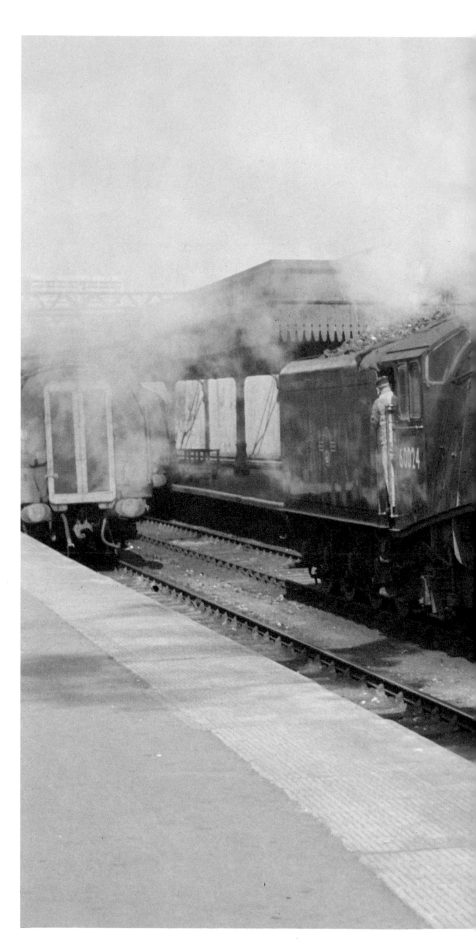

A4 60024 backing on to 13.30 to Glasgow - 27 August 1966

Mike
Vincent

BRITISH RAILWAY
STEAM
in Colour

ARGUS BOOKS

Argus Books
Argus House
Boundary Way
Hemel Hempstead
Herts HP2 7ST
England
First published by Argus Books 1992

ISBN 1 85486 073 9

Phototypesetting by Island Graphics, Chesham
Design by D & P Associates, Chesham
Printed and bound in Great Britain by William Clowes Ltd., Beccles

CONTENTS

Introduction

B.C. or Before Colour

Railway photography has long been a main line interest of the railway enthusiast. Without it much of the history and record of not just British railways, but also those across the world, would have passed and been totally lost. Today, the availability of equipment and film, technically beyond belief to the enthusiast of only 40 years ago, ensures that much more is recorded by the humble, and often much maligned, enthusiast.

As a child and right through my teens, my interest in trains, both prototype and model, was almost to the exclusion of everything else, including my education, and gave rise at times to considerable parental concern. The spur to take a morning paper round was the freedom given, by the money earned, to travel to various rail centres and of course, to stand around on the station platform the entire day. In the short period between the end of the Second World War and the nationalisation of the railways, I spent almost every weekend watching and travelling on trains. Living in Finchley in North London, it was also possible to cycle to a great variety of

Neasden locomotive shed was within easy reach by bicycle and during one visit LNER Class M2, 0-6-4T (ex-Metropolitan Railway) No 9076 *Robert H Selbie* posed in front of the Kodak Brownie box camera - 17 May 1947.

A brand new LNER B1 Class 4-6-0, No 1142 at Neasden locomotive shed in LNER post-war apple green. The locomotive is standing alongside a water column with its heating brazier to avoid freezing up in winter. Every water column of the thousands across the country had its brazier and every brazier had to be maintained throughout the winter months - 17 May 1947.

The third of the trio of locomotives included from Neasden locomotive shed in May 1947 is LNER K3 Class 2-6-0, No 1824. No apple green livery for this engine which is still in its wartime livery, with the LNER on the tender reduced down to just NE - 24 May 1947.

From Neasden locomotive shed I used my bicycle to reach the Great Western at Old Oak Common where, outside the repair shop, I recorded an Old Oak Common curiosity. A half-cab 0-6-0PT, No 1912, built in 1882, which survived until 1949 and 47 years older than any other pannier tank allocated to the shed when this photograph was taken - 26 April 1947.

railway vantage points. There were a number of major locomotive sheds accessible to a fit lad with a bicycle - the LMS at Cricklewood on the ex-Midland line; Neasden on the old Great Central route of the LNER; a stop at Willesden, again for the LMS and finally Old Oak Common for the Great Western. An early start with some sandwiches and a bottle of Tizer and all these could be covered within the day. The day would close by watching the Great Western parade in the late afternoon sunset from the staff footbridge at the throat of Old Oak Common shed and carriage sidings. I used my bicycle to the limit in order to save money for the special trips and also in this period, for film.

The longer journeys by bicycle included a ride to Shoeburyness, which was not a success on three counts. First, the station and shed only yielded standard LMS tanks to view. Second, the tide was out on a very hot day and there was no chance for a swim. Third, we - there were two for company that day - missed a turning in east London on the way back and put some miles on our journey. However, a trip to Hitchin is remembered with much greater pleasure despite the problem of cycling up seemingly endless hills on the journey. Today it is impossible to appreciate the country junction atmosphere that existed in Hitchin in the late 1940s.

As an aside, and to put rail travel of the era into perspective, let me relate a personal experience which took place some years later during the early BR diesel period. I was travelling to Spalding from Kings Cross by an early morning train and met an acquaintance in the restaurant car. He was only going as far as Hitchin and yet, such was the pace of rail travel then, he comfortably ordered, was served, ate and paid for his breakfast in time to alight at Hitchin. He had kippers, I seem to remember.

Going back to the 1940s, my early morning paper round provided the funds for day trips by rail. The timing of the express trains of those days was clearly pedestrian with a 60mph maximum speed generally prevailing. The practical limit of a day trip was less than 100 miles, bearing in mind that the object of the trip was to spend some time at the destination and not just travelling. I visited all the major rail centres, some more than once, together with many more minor centres - it was a hit and miss affair. Obviously Swindon and Works visits guaranteed plenty of interest and a worthwhile day. The same applied to Peterborough, March, Bletchley and Salisbury. Other visits such as to Three Bridges and Horsham were disappointing but that may have been due to being in the depths of the appalling winter of 1946/47. In the same area, Guildford was full of interest and rewarding. How different it all is today with a rail system that is no longer freight orientated. Where, for example, is the day long interest at March today?

With all these weekend perambulations, I started to carry a camera, the very basic of photographic devices - a Kodak Brownie box camera. Memory says that they sold for 5/- (25p) each before the Second World War. That, of course, needs to be put into context, as a family camera, even at that price, was far from being a common household object. Then, as now, a camera needs endowment. Film and processing was nowhere near as cheap, relatively speaking, as it is today. Furthermore, you only received a print the same size as the negative. Hence, the popularity of the 120 film which at least gave you a basic print large enough for individuals to be recognised from snaps taken on holiday.

Equipped as I was with such a basic camera, my early railway photographs also came within the category of 'snaps'. There was also an additional problem. During the immediate post-war years, film was an unknown quantity. Quantities of surplus war stock were sold on the retail market, but this would often have a row of sprocket holes across the top of the film - a hazard not apparent until the film was returned after being developed. In company with, no doubt, many a headless Mum and Dad on holiday, I found I had locomotives without chimneys and domes. However I persevered and gradually a small collection of reasonable photographs was established. Today they seem to be from a different age - not only because some of the locomotives photographed would not have survived as long as they did if it had not been for the war, but today the images of many of those negatives have all but faded away. Fortunately, in the early 1960s I realised what was happening and had some rephotographed to form 2 ¼ inch square transparencies and a few of the best enlarged as a record of my teens. From these I have selected a few to illustrate the adventures of a teenager and a box camera. The captions say the rest.

In company with the rest of my generation, I was conscripted for National Service. The spring of 1950 found Gunner Vincent, Trigonometrical Surveyor (RA), as a member of 'X' troop of the 94th Observation Regt RA, based in Luneburg, Germany. The freedom of the six survey pairs in that unit, each with their own jeep and trailer, was beyond belief for the average conscripted National Serviceman. Particularly as,

A holiday in the Lake District gave rise to an opportunity to visit Barrow-in-Furness locomotive shed where LMS (ex-L&NWR) 0-6-0, No 28128 was caught while being prepared for duty. Note the tool box is open and the fall plate between engine and tender has been lifted up. Barrow suffered heavily from bombing raids during the war and the shed did not escape - 26 August 1947.

Last of the photographs included which was taken by the Kodak Brownie box camera. With the railways nationalised at the beginning of the year this locomotive was now ex-GWR 44XX Class 2-6-2T, No 4407 at Plymouth, North Road Station - 19 August 1948.

after the start of the Korean War on 25 June 1950, BAOR was very much on a war footing. Each of the survey pairs, equipped with a simple arm band, was untouchable - even, as I personally discovered, by such a worthy as the Office i/c of the Military Police for an armoured division. All this may seem to be totally irrelevant to the context of this book - but read on.

On arrival in Germany, being paid a wage of 7/- (35p) a day, I was determined that, if nothing else, I would go home with a decent camera. Decent cameras were only available for deutsche marks and at that time there was no way that you could exchange sterling for marks. I gradually accumulated a small hoard of marks by selling my cigarette ration to other members of the unit, usually regulars acting as a kind of middleman. They had been around for years and had built on a small network of contacts, often through the German civilians employed on the camp. When the Korean War started things looked serious, particularly when your viewpoint was only some 12 or 13 miles from the East German border. What was even more serious was the possibility of a decent camera being lost as well!

I made a decision. I added up the German marks and purchased the best possible camera. It was not what I had hoped to buy, but the Agfa Isolette V has done me noble service and has been used for all the colour photographs in this book. I had bought a camera far in advance of the Box

Brownie, but with a maximum aperture of 4.5 and shutter speed of 1/200 it still established very limiting constraints when using colour some 15 years later. Even so, I now had a camera which greatly extended the range of railway photography over that previously available to me by a quantum leap. Against this, the opportunities for photography were far less. Basically, these were limited to the locomotive depot at Luneburg. A British soldier actually asking permission to go around the shed was clearly a novelty as it was still a time when it was common for German civilians to step off the pavement to let you pass. For someone who was used to the condition of British locomotive sheds in the post-war years, Luneburg shed was an eye-opener. It was spotless. Dirty windows did not exist, not even those alternating with the smoke vents to the roof of the roundhouse.

As most who experienced service in the forces, a gulf had been created on return to civilian life. You did not simply carry on where you had left off. In addition, it became apparent that basically the Agfa was a pre-war camera carried over into the post-war era. Railway photography became a random affair in that I did not seek out the subject specifically to photograph it - that is, not until I acquired a cine camera. Overnight, railway photography became a whole new ball game, as no doubt anyone who has acquired a camcorder will have discovered. The cine camera was technically well ahead of the old Agfa in that it had an automatic aperture, the shutter speed being fixed. Once more I spent weekends at stations and

'Luneburg shed was an eye-opener. It was spotless. Dirty windows did not exist, not even those alternating with the smoke vent to the roof of the roundhouse.'
Luneburg, West Germany, showing Baltic 4-6-4 tank, No 78521 on turntable outside roundhouse - summer 1951.

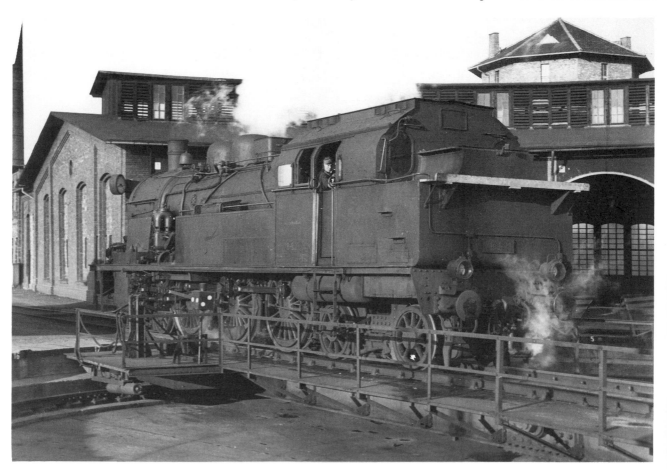

lineside venues with the cine camera and the Agfa (still with black and white film). I soon realised that the Agfa produced a good still record of the cine coverage and obtained some very satisfying results.

By now I had been potting away at railways with black and white film for nearly twenty years. Once the monochrome prints were enlarged, preferably to 'whole plate' size, then I could enjoy each photograph. For generations the railway enthusiast had used monochrome film and many refused to move away to colour. Today it might seem faintly ridiculous, but when you could get a whole plate enlargement for the same cost as a 2 ¼ inch square transparency, there did appear to be sound reasons. Further, as I explain later, the change did not immediately guarantee photographs to the same quality.

I continued in this way until the friendly local camera shop encouraged me to try colour transparencies, something I had previously discounted on the grounds of cost. My belief in the excessive cost of transparencies had been lodged in the days of my first job, before Army

Ex-LNER A4 Class 4-6-2 Pacific, BR No 60022 *Mallard* at Waterloo on a commemoration special run of the 1948 locomotive trials. Taken as a supporting black and white while filming with the cine camera. This was definitely one that I wished I had on colour film.

Service, when I earned a mere £2 per week. One lunch hour I made a trip to Wallace Heaton solely to gaze in their window. At that time they were promoting 35mm slides and had examples in the window. I seem to remember that the sales pitch was 'Only 2/3d (11p) per slide for the film, developing and mounting'. Only! That was two weeks take-home pay for one roll of 36 exposures!

The friendly local camera shop, with an eye to business, persisted but my first purchase of a roll of 120 Kodachrome was an unmitigated disaster. In an attempt to save the situation, the shop proposed an affordable secondhand light meter and I made another attempt, with sufficiently successful results for colour transparencies to be permanently kept in the faithful old Agfa. It was not all plain sailing as the Kodachrome of those days, with an ASA rating of only 64 used with a maximum aperture of 4.5, required good light for locomotive subjects. While a move to Ektachrome and Ektachrome High Speed increased the opportunities for photography, they could result in very thin colour in the transparencies at times. Then, as now I have to admit, signal posts and lamp standards would mysteriously sprout from chimneys and domes. In fact, I had to start again and give each exposure a lot more thought than with black and white.

Unlike many other recorders of the railway scene, who concentrated on a particular, and often local, line giving an in-depth record, I was (and still am) very much of an itinerant when it came to railway photography. Again, in the 1960s as in the 1940s, the film was made to last. After all, it was still very much a record of the main feature which was the cine. As a result, no particular item was ever swamped. For example, a weekend visit to the Lickey Incline only had one roll of 12 exposures expended but, the

A type of GWR designed pannier tank which was not built in large numbers, 15XX Class 0-6-0PT, No 1506. Seen here backing out of Paddington Station, having brought empty stock into the station earlier. These were powerful tank engines but only 10 were built, all by BR in 1949 after nationalisation. The wheel base was reduced to the minimum possible allowing the locomotives to traverse curves as sharp as 3 chains. On withdrawal, they were seen as an ideal industrial locomotive by the National Coal Board. Unfortunately, they overlooked the fact that they were the heaviest of the GWR 0-6-0PTs built. The havoc they wrought on the type of track illustrated later in this book resulted in a very short working after-life.

Ex-GWR Hall Class 4-6-0, No 5990 *Dorford Hall* with an up fitted freight taking the through road at Oxford station - 26 April 1963.

cine was allocated a much larger budget. Consequently, the format of this book has been fashioned by the dictates of my personal financial restrictions of nearly 30 years ago.

I have made a selection which I hope will illustrate to every reader a section of British Railways that they are familiar with, or have had knowledge of. It is set out in a gentle perambulation around the country. Basically, only the South West and Wales do not receive coverage, for which I apologize. The sections vary in coverage, but each are complete in themselves. Open anywhere you like and I hope that your attention is caught and interest held on every page.

**Standard BR 9F 2-10-0
locomotive No 92089 backing
into Leicester locomotive shed -
12 November 1963.**

'... name plate and the replica coat of arms which showed that someone still found the time to polish the brasswork.'
Name plate on rebuilt West Country Class Pacific at Nine Elms - 4 September 1965.

SOUTHERN AT NINE ELMS

For our gentle perambulation around the country, I decided that our starting point would be Waterloo. However, before the train could leave Waterloo, it was necessary for Nine Elms locomotive depot to roster a suitable engine for the trip. The Southern Railway was way behind the other three pre-nationalisation railway companies when it came to the size of its steam locomotive stock. Even so, Nine Elms was one of London's major locomotive depots. It therefore seemed logical that the first section should start at Nine Elms rather than Waterloo.

On a visit to Nine Elms, the first locomotives to catch the eye had to be the various Bulleid Pacifics. Almost to the end of steam out of Waterloo, they were turned out as clean as they could be with the shed difficulties and labour shortages of the 1960s. Opposite is a view of a rebuilt West Country Class Pacific 4-6-2, BR No 34018 *Axminster* on 4 September 1965. Not only does this shot bear out my comment on the presentation of these engines, it also illustrates the appalling working conditions under which these engines were maintained.

On this page is a close-up of *Axminster's* name plate and the replica coat of arms which showed that someone still found the time to polish the brasswork. It is also a close-up of one of the archaic and labour-intensive operating practices that prevailed on British Railways to the end of steam. The capped tube to the right of the name plate is the filler pipe for sand. This was required to sand the rails in the event of the driving wheels not having sufficient adhesion. I am not a small man but it can be seen that the filler cap is some way above my head. This was filled from the sand furnace and hoisted up by hand by one member of the crew to another standing on the footplate, it was then tipped into sandboxes placed below the boiler to catch any water that may have leaked. In America the sand was obtained by pipe from an overhead bin into a sandbox on top of the boiler where it was kept warm and dry.

In an even better condition externally, was another rebuilt West Country, BR No 34040 *Crewkerne* when I visited the shed on 10 August 1963. From the look of the thin blast of smoke at the chimney, the blower is on in order to raise steam for the locomotive's next turn of duty. Locomotives coming on to the shed were generally turned to face the shed.

'... the first locomotives to catch the eye had to be the various Bulleid Pacifics.' Ex-Southern Railway rebuilt West Country Class 4-6-2 Pacific, BR No 34018 *Axminster* at Nine Elms locomotive shed - 4 September 1965.

'... the blower is on in order to raise steam for the locomotive's next turn of duty.' Ex-Southern Railway rebuilt West Country Class 4-6-2 Pacific, BR No 34040 *Crewkerne* at Nine Elms locomotive shed - 10 August 1963.

All locomotive movements on and off the shed had to make use of the turntable. It was possible to avoid the turntable by shunting up and down the yard each time tacking across to avoid the turntable. Locomotives rostered to take trains out of Waterloo would not need the use of the turntable again, should it break down, just extra time to leave the yard.

Having caught up with the more impressive locomotives on shed, what else would have been found on a typical visit? Ex-Southern Railway U Class 2-6-0, BR No 31790 was formerly the first locomotive of the South Eastern & Chatham Railway's K or River Class 2-6-4Ts and carried the name *River Avon*. During the 1920s and under Southern Railway ownership, they were all rebuilt as shown. As tank engines, they were designed for fast expresses between London and the Kent coast and this passenger role was still recognised by British Rail and given lined black livery. The coaling plant in the background was enormous and towered over everything. I have no comparative details but it must surely have been one of the largest in the country.

Empty stock workings, in and out of Waterloo, were an endless requirement. They were lengthy as the carriage sidings were some 6 or 7 miles down the line. Once the old London & South Western Railway M7 Class 0-4-4T engines were withdrawn, Nine Elms rostered anything that moved for these duties. On shed on 4 September 1965 was one of the BR Standard Class 3, 2-6-2T locomotives, No 82006. During the early 1960s BR realised that the stock of green paint was far greater than needed for locomotives designated to receive green livery. For a while, all types of

'... formerly the first locomotive of the South Eastern & Chatham Railway's K or River Class 2-6-4Ts ...'
Ex-Southern Railway U Class 2-6-0, BR No 31790 at Nine Elms - 10 August 1963.

'For a while all types of unlikely locomotive classes appeared in green livery ...'
BR Standard Class 3, 2-6-2T locomotive, No 82006 at Nine Elms - 4 September 1965.

'Only the name plate is missing to give any indication that this engine was no longer in service ...'
Ex-Southern Railway Schools Class 4-4-0, BR No 30903 *Charterhouse* at Nine Elms locomotive shed - 10 August 1963.

unlikely locomotive classes appeared in green livery, instead of the expected black. I cannot recall seeing any other of these Class 3, 2-6-2T engines in green, but then there were only 45 locomotives in the class. On the other hand, green was a very appropriate livery for a Swindon design of engine.

One class which was designated to receive green livery was the ex-Southern Railway Schools Class 4-4-0. Technically the class was withdrawn from service at the end of 1962, but BR No 30903 *Charterhouse* was still on shed on 10 August 1963. Only the name plate is missing to give any indication that this engine was no longer in service, but that cannot detract from what was, to me, the most stylish 4-4-0 on British rails.

From beauty to the beast and the supposed result of coping with wartime shortages. I do not believe that any of the Bulleid ex-Southern Railway Q1 Class 0-6-0s were ever painted other than in black. BR No 33009 was one of only 40 locomotives, none of which seemed to stray from old Southern Railway metals. They were ugly and powerful brutes. They also had that most desirable feature of freight engines - their brakes worked! This was demonstrated to me when travelling from Reading to Redhill; the locomotive rostered for the duty was Q1 No 33020. The line into Dorking Town descends a gradient of 1 in 96 and 1 in 100. Coming down the bank at 45-50 mph, I thought that we were going to run straight through. Not until the engine was only yards from the platform did the brakes go on and I was treated to a braking demonstration I would not experience again until British Rail went over to airbraking on their stock.

Time to make our way from the shed to Waterloo and find an ex-Southern Railway rebuilt Merchant Navy Class 4-6-2 Pacific, BR No 35021 *New Zealand Line* under the coaling stage. My observation of working at Nine Elms showed that locomotives always coaled as they left the shed. Most of the coaling stage is masked by the steam blowing off from 35021 but obvious in the foreground is that barrow of sand. This was referred to in my comments on the close-up of the name plate on *Axminster*. This picture says more than any number of words on the subject of waste, poor practice and unproductive labour with which the operating departments had to contend.

From the shed there was a short sharp climb on a curve up to a lay-by on the main line. Here locomotives would wait for the right away into Waterloo. Locomotives coming onto shed from Waterloo would usually be held until there were two or three to make the trip together. Going up to

'... the supposed result of coping with wartime shortages.' Ex-Southern Railway Q1 Class 0-6-0, BR No 33009 at Nine Elms locomotive shed - 4 September 1965.

'My observation of working at Nine Elms showed that locomotives always coaled as they left the shed.' Ex-Southern Railway rebuilt Merchant Navy Class 4-6-2 Pacific, BR No 35021 *New Zealand Line* under the coaling stage at Nine Elms locomotive shed - 10 August 1963.

'The array of running lines, in and out of Waterloo, are spread out in front of the camera ...' BR Standard Class 4, 2-6-0 No 76066 with an up semi-fast from Basingstoke passing Nine Elms Loco Box - 10 August 1963.

Waterloo, they made the run singly. The shed had its own signal box, known as 'Nine Elms Loco Box' just to handle this traffic and the final scene in this section was taken from the footplate of S15 Class 4-6-0, No 30838 while waiting by Nine Elms Loco Box for the working run up to Waterloo on 10 August 1963. The array of running lines, in and out of Waterloo, are spread out in front of the camera, and in the centre is BR Standard Class 4, 2-6-0, No 76066 with an up semi-fast from Basingstoke. The S15 I was on would follow this train into the platform at Waterloo for a return working back to Basingstoke.

WATERLOO

British Rail ran an intensive steam service out of Waterloo station right up until the electrification of the Bournemouth line was commissioned. Only the route to the South West through Salisbury and Exeter suffered the demise of steam seen on other lines, through a step-by-step introduction of diesel power. Granted, at the very end, the exterior condition of both the locomotives and rolling stock fell off noticeably, as only basic safety and operating maintenance was carried out pending the introduction of new motive power and stock, but the intense timetable was still kept. Because of the steam facilities that were still available, both at Waterloo and Nine Elms, Waterloo became a regular starting point for enthusiasts' specials. The last photograph in the previous section was taken from the footplate of an S15 Class 4-6-0. As that locomotive was not shown, I have started with two views of another member of the S15 Class, booked to take out an enthusiasts' special. The date was 16 January 1966 and the first shot shows No 30837 backing down into Waterloo station with the tracks still covered from a light fall of snow. Nine Elms locomotive shed had made a

'... became a regular starting point for enthusiasts' specials.' Ex-Southern Railway S15 Class 4-6-0, BR No 30837, backing into Waterloo station preparatory to hauling a commemoration run for the S15 Class - 16 January 1966.

superb job of presenting the locomotive for the special. Everything about No 30837 shone. Not only did the copper and brass pipework sparkle but there was also a great deal of bright steelwork.

On arrival at Waterloo, No 30837 backed into the locomotive servicing bay, where the station pilots waited between duties. The second shot shows her standing in this servicing bay and the full extent of the bright steelwork is evident. Somebody had worked very hard, on a very cold morning, in turning out this engine.

From specials to the mundane everyday working and the most modern form of steam motive power working in and out of Waterloo - a rebuilt West Country. Shown on 14 August 1965, No 34005 *Barnstaple* is backing out of the arrival platform having been released from the train it had brought up to Waterloo. Built in July 1945 as Southern Railway No 21C105, *Barnstaple* was rebuilt into the form shown here in June 1957. When this photograph was taken, August 1965, she only had another 14 months of work left, being withdrawn in October 1966.

'... and the full extent of the bright steelwork is evident.' Ex-Southern Railway S15 Class 4-6-0, BR No 30837 standing in engine service bay at Waterloo station prior to hauling an enthuslasts' special - 16 January 1966.

'... backing out of the arrival platform having been released from the train it had brought up to Waterloo.' Ex-Southern Railway rebuilt West Country Class 4-6-2 Pacific, BR No 34005 *Barnstaple* at Waterloo - 14 August 1965.

'Crew protection from the weather had received a good deal of thought on this class of locomotive ...'
Cab of ex-Southern Railway rebuilt Battle of Britain Class 4-6-2 Pacific, BR No 34056 *Croydon* at Waterloo - 26 November 1966.

'The opportunity is also taken to show the name plate and crest ...'
Name plate and crest on ex-Southern Railway rebuilt Battle of Britain Class 4-6-2 Pacific, BR No 34056 *Croydon* at Waterloo - 26 November 1966.

Waterloo was the location of the cameo showing the faintly embarrassed driver sitting in his cab waiting for the right away. The locomotive was a Battle of Britain variant of a rebuilt West Country, No 34056 *Croydon* and the date 26 November 1966. Crew protection from the weather had received a good deal of thought on this class of locomotive, with a well-designed, flexible connection between cab and tender. During the journeys recorded in the following pages it will become evident just how far advanced was Bulleid, the designer of this class of engine, in his provision of weather protection for the crew. The opportunity is also taken to show the name plate and crest of No 34056 *Croydon* as a comparison with the name plate on *Axminster* seen at Nine Elms earlier.

An earlier photograph showed S15 No 30837 had run into the small locomotive servicing bay. A shot has been included of BR Standard Class 3, 2-6-2T locomotive No 82019 standing in the bay, taking on water. Even at Waterloo, there seemed to be time for anyone and everyone to stop and watch an everyday operation. The gallows contraption in front of the engine, was an old loading gauge. This, I believe, was installed from days when wagonloads of freight were accepted as an everyday event making the need for a loading gauge a necessity.

Before travelling down the line, here is an illustration of an operating practice already mentioned in connection with Nine Elms. The last scene in this section shows rebuilt Merchant Navy Class 4-6-2 Pacific, BR No 35007 *Aberdeen Commonwealth* and rebuilt Battle of Britain Class 4-6-2, No 34060 *25 Squadron* coupled together. These engines had earlier brought up trains to Waterloo and were waiting to travel to Nine Elms locomotive shed in tandem. It was almost impossible to tell the difference visually between these two classes of locomotive, even when coupled together, much less when apart. Make no mistake though, the Merchant Navy Class was a vastly superior locomotive when it came to power and haulage. This comment has not been made on the basis that the nominal tractive effort of the Merchant Navy Class was more than 20% greater, but from talking to drivers of the day. They had no illusions as to which class they preferred to be driving. Clearly doubting my intelligence, in that I should mention both classes in the same breath, one driver unequivocally stated that there was no comparison.

'... seemed to be time for anyone and everyone to stop and watch an everyday operation.'
BR Standard Class 3, 2-6-2T locomotive, No 82019 at Waterloo - 14 August 1965.

'Clearly doubting my intelligence, in that I should mention both classes in the same breath ...'
Ex-Southern Railway rebuilt 4-6-2 Pacific Merchant Navy Class BR No 35007 *Aberdeen Commonwealth* and No 34060 *25 Squadron* at Waterloo - 14 August 1965.

WINCHESTER SURPRISE

For a period of eighteen months or so, Winchester was on my way home. Come the summer and the light evenings, I decided to investigate the photographic possibilities of the station. Today, it is almost impossible to appreciate the freedom a car still gave in the early 1960s, particularly as on every time I visited Winchester I parked in the station approach which was still legal and possible without hassle. If it had not been so easy to park, I doubt if I would have persevered in stopping. After three or four visits using the southern end of the station for a vantage point, with very disappointing results, I decided to try my luck from the north end of the up platform.

Typical of the trains available to be photographed on that and other visits, is illustrated in the introduction to this section. Shown is an inter-region service, one of the longest at the time, the Newcastle-Bournemouth on 29 August 1963. In charge of the train is BR-built Great Western Hall Class 4-6-0, No 7911 *Lady Margaret Hall* with a rake of Southern Region coaches which must have looked most out of place if they had been run right through to Newcastle.

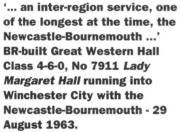

'... an inter-region service, one of the longest at the time, the Newcastle-Bournemouth ...' BR-built Great Western Hall Class 4-6-0, No 7911 *Lady Margaret Hall* running into Winchester City with the Newcastle-Bournemouth - 29 August 1963.

'This, at the time, did not seem possible, I thought the entire class had been withdrawn.'
Ex-L&SWR B4 Class 0-4-0T, BR No 30102 in goods yard at Winchester City - 29 August 1963.

Conditions were not a great deal better than the down end of the station as the light in the early evening was deteriorating and the down trains were still moving at some speed as they approached the station. I had been there for some time and was on the verge of calling it a day, when I turned and idly gazed across the goods yard behind the up platform station buildings. There, sitting in the smallest of locomotive sheds, was an ex-L&SWR B4 Class 0-4-0T, BR No 30102. This, at the time, did not seem possible - I thought the entire class had been withdrawn. I was wrong, but only just, in that the record books show that No 30102 went within a matter of days. I promptly left the station, the exit being of course from the opposite side of the line, and made my way round, by road, to the goods yard. Panic! I found that it was well and truly locked up for the night. Back to the station where I was directed to the station foreman. This individual clearly knew more about public relations than many actually in that position, because he found the key and a member of his staff to accompany me back into the goods yard.

The efforts of that evening produced two of my most satisfying photographs. The smallest of sub-sheds with an 0-4-0T that filled the inside of the shed totally. It was recording gems like this that made the near misses and failures all worthwhile.

'The smallest of sub-sheds with an 0-4-0T that filled the inside of the shed totally.'
Ex-L&SWR B4 Class 0-4-0T, BR No 30102 in goods yard at Winchester City - 29 August 1963.

SOUTHERN MOGULS

Duuring the days of steam haulage, there always seemed to be more opportunities than there are today to stop and photograph an interesting railway subject. The opportunities were made that more easy because if I was travelling by car and saw something of interest there was generally no problem in parking and investigating. Typical of the results of these opportunities were the two scenes which illustrate this section.

The first arose while I was bumping across the level crossing at Toton on the afternoon of 10 July 1963. I saw an engine quietly simmering away nearby. Parking the trusty MGA outside the shops immediately beyond the crossing was no problem at all and picking up the camera, I walked back to see what was to be found. It turned out to be an ex-Southern Railway U Class Mogul 2-6-0, BR No 31806 and the first photograph was taken leaning over the level crossing gates. Why this engine was there has never been apparent. There was no crew visible – in fact, no railway staff whatsoever.

' ... it was the Southern mogul as exemplified here, that handled so much of the semi-fast traffic on the old Southern ... '
Ex-Southern Railway U Class Mogul 2-6-0, BR No 31806 at Toton – 10 July 1963.

Originally No 31806 was a K Class 2-6-4T, Southern Railway No. 806 *River Torridge*, built at Brighton in 1926. Prior to 1960, it was the Southern mogul, as exemplified here, that handled so much of the semi-fast traffic on the old Southern and early years of the Southern Region. Officially the U Class moguls were limited to a maximum speed of 70 miles per hour. Such a restriction though would not be a handicap when a typical semi-fast of the period would be allowed 2 hours 37 minutes for only 83.75 miles from Salisbury to Waterloo with four intermediate stops.

The second scene shows the south end of Guildford station on 22 September 1965. This photograph was another case of stopping the car near a railway bridge just to see if there was anything of interest. Once again I was rewarded by the sight of an ex-Southern Railway N Class 2-6-0, BR No 31866. The origins and design of this efficient and modern-looking engine were not a product of Eastleigh, but originated during Maunsell's regime on the pre-group South Eastern & Chatham at Ashford. Shown here it is probably difficult to appreciate that, when built in May 1925, this particular locomotive was exhibited by the Southern Railway at the British Empire Exhibition, Wembley, until November of that year.

No 31866 remained in the station long enough for me to arrive on the platform to record her departure on cine film. The locomotive had been brought to a stand, with her cylinders in dead centre. On the driver opening the regulator nothing happened, so he started to wind the engine into reverse. As he did so, the train started to roll backwards. Immediately, the driver began to wind the reverser into forward gear again as fast as he could without applying the brakes. The engine not only took the train off immediately but, as can still be seen from the film that recorded this episode, gave a superb display of acceleration in the process.

' … when built in May 1925, this particular locomotive was exhibited by the Southern Railway at the British Empire Exhibition, Wembley, until November of that year.'
Ex-Southern Railway N Class 2-6-0, BR No 31866 at Guildford – 22 September 1965.

SOUTHERN RAILS IN THE COUNTRY

The illustrations which form this section were taken during the occasional coffee break on long journeys. Of course they did not happen by chance and, in order to have a coffee break, a vacuum flask of coffee was necessary. My travels fell into set routines and once the route was established, suitable railway orientated halts were noted. This was at a time before the motorway network had gridded the country, and a modicum of map-reading soon established the best possible 15 minute halts.

Typical of these halts was that at Micheldever, just a matter of minutes off the A30 and on the main line from London to Bournemouth. It was here on a cold and frosty 3 January in 1967 that I photographed the first two illustrations. The engine was an ex-Southern Railway rebuilt West Country 4-6-2 Pacific, BR No 34044 *Woolacombe*. Whatever these pictures have lost on account of the unkempt appearance of the engine is more than made up for by the crisp exhaust accentuated by the below-freezing temperature.

' ... on the main line from London to Bournemouth.' Ex-Southern Railway rebuilt West Country Class 4-6-2 Pacific, BR No 34044 *Woolacombe* with a down express just south of Micheldever – 3 January 1967.

'Whatever these pictures have lost on account of the unkempt appearance of the engine is more than made up for by the crisp exhaust ...'
Ex-Southern Railway rebuilt West Country Class 4-6-2 Pacific, BR No 34044 *Woolacombe* with a down oxpross just south of Micheldever – 3 January 1967.

'This outwardly unpromising section of line yielded a sighting of a Fareham to Cardiff train ... '
BR Standard Class 4, 2-6-0 locomotive No 76067 on a Fareham to Cardiff cross-country train near North Baddesley, between Eastleigh and Romsey – 2 March 1965.

From Micheldever to a spot near North Baddesley, a small village between Eastleigh and Romsey. This outwardly unpromising section of line yielded a sighting of a Fareham to Cardiff train on 2 March 1965. Headed by BR Standard Class 4, 2-6-0, No 76067, the second coach of the train was interesting because it was one of the few which Western Region had painted in the old Great Western chocolate and cream for use on limited main line expresses.

My route from North Baddesley to Beaulieu Road in the New Forest actually took me past Beaulieu Road station. At times in the year when it would have been too dark by the time I reached Winchester, I would have an early tea break in the New Forest. I have included three scenes; the first taken on 27 February 1964. This shows a typical Southern Region express of the period in full flight across the New Forest. Headed by ex-Southern Railway rebuilt West Country Class 4-6-2 Pacific, No. 34040 *Crewkerne* on a down Bournemouth express, it would have been an exhilarating moment as the train passed.

Some five or six weeks later on 9 April, a similar stop produced records of two more passing trains. The first was an old friend of the period, the *Pines Express*. Probably as a result of the advanced warning given by the signal seen just beyond the fourth coach, I had moved nearer the line for this train than that shown previously. This time the engine is an original West Country Class 4-6-2 Pacific, BR No 34105 *Swanage*.

To conclude this section of trains in the country, another from 9 April 1964 near Beaulieu Road. An up fitted freight train of assorted vans, headed by an unidentified member of the BR Standard 75XXX Class 4, 4-6-0 mixed traffic locomotives. Freight trains marshalled like this and headed by another mixed traffic 4-6-0 were seen constantly and like most other enthusiasts of the day, I normally just watched them roll past. Fortunately, on 9 April 1964 I took a little more interest than normal.

' ... a typical Southern Region express of the period in full flight across the New Forest.' Ex-Southern Railway rebuilt West Country Class 4-6-2 Pacific, No 34040 *Crewkerne* approaching Beaulieu Road with a down Bournemouth express – 27 February 1964.

' ... an old friend of the period, the *Pines Express*.'
Ex-Southern Railway original West Country Class 4-6-2 Pacific, BR No 34105 *Swanage* approaching Beaulieu Road with the Bournemouth *Pines Express* – 9 April 1964.

'Freight trains marshalled like this and headed by another mixed traffic 4-6-0 were seen constantly ... '
BR Standard 75XXX Class 4, 4-6-0 locomotive with an up fitted freight near Beaulieu Road – 9 April 1964.

THE LYMINGTON BRANCH

There are three recognised routes to the Isle of Wight from the mainland: Portsmouth to Ryde, Southampton to Cowes and Lymington Pier to Yarmouth. In my many visits to the island I have used all three. Portsmouth to Ryde always seemed to be mass transit in action, particularly in the holiday season. In the days of travel by sea and the great liners, Southampton to Cowes was, for me, the most interesting. The third, from Lymington Pier to Yarmouth – well, that was very different.

Lymington Pier was at the end of the archetypal branch line which left the Southern main line between Southampton and Bournemouth, just beyond Brockenhurst. There is, because the line is still open, only one intermediate station on the branch, Lymington Town, and when the photographs in this section were taken, this line encapsulated all the charm that has become part of branch line lore. To set the mood and establish the atmosphere, I have included a picture of the station from the forecourt as it appeared on 16 January 1964 – all gables and lofty chimney stacks. Imagine, as you walk across the forecourt, that it is the cover of a book that you are about to open.

' ... all gables and lofty chimney stacks.'
Lymington Station from the forecourt – 16 January 1964.

' ... standing in the platform at the head of a two-coach train to Brockenhurst.'
L&SWR, ex-Southern Railway M7 0-4-4T, BR No 30108 standing at the platform of Lymington Town – 16 January 1964.

' ... an engine which has probably been working the branch all week and yet the coal bunker is so full, the coal is piled high on the cab roof.'
Ex-L&SWR, ex-SR, M7 0-4-4T, BR No 30108 leaving Lymington Town for Brockenhurst – 16 January 1964.

Through the ticket office and onto the platform and you would have found ex-Southern Railway M7 Class 0-4-4T, BR No 30108 standing in the platform at the head of a two-coach train to Brockenhurst. Built in March 1904, it was only two months away from its 60th birthday, an event which it only survived for a further two months, being withdrawn in May 1964. Noteworthy about the first photograph of 30108, is the overall station roof complete with smoke vent.

The next photograph shows 30108 leaving the station on the way to Brockenhurst with Lymington Town locomotive shed in the background. This scene shows a remarkable feature of 30108. Here we have an engine which has probably been working the branch all week and yet the coal bunker is so full that the coal is piled high on the cab roof. As can be seen from the following photographs, the shed only boasted a coaling platform and the mystery of the coal on the cab roof was only explained when, some time later, I was privileged to some cab rides. It was then I discovered that a small pile of coal was left between the tracks in the station. The driver carefully stopped the cab alongside the pile of coal, and the fireman dropped to the ground and furiously shovelled enough coal onto the cab floor for another round trip to Brockenhurst. This fascinating piece of railway operation, not found in the rule book, I subsequently recorded with the cine camera.

The small shed seen behind 30108, is shown in greater detail in the next two scenes. Two different dates and two different locomotives – although both the same class. The first was taken on 27 November 1963, and shows ex-Southern Railway Q Class 0-6-0, BR No 30535 built in September 1938 and withdrawn in April 1965. The second was taken on 16 January 1964 and shows No 30546 of the same class, built in June 1939 and withdrawn, just four months after the photograph was taken, in May 1964. In the first the coaling platform can be seen showing the implausibility of getting coal on the cab roof of the M7, No 30108. In each case these locomotives are seen shunting the small yard which operation required the locomotive and wagons to pass right through the shed.

The final photograph was taken from the footplate of a 2-6-2T, BR No 41224 on 26 February 1965. This engine was from a class of locomotive introduced by the London Midland & Scottish Railway just after World War Two. When, in May 1964, the M7 0-4-4T shown in the previous shots was withdrawn, along with seven or eight others of that class still surviving, they were replaced on the Lymington Branch by the ex-LM&SR 2-6-2 Tanks. The 2-6-2Ts were not auto-fitted so the locomotive had to run round its train at each end of the journey. My notes do not record where on the branch this particular photograph was taken, however, as my presence on the footplate was tolerated on the strict understanding I did not step onto the driver's side of the cab, it had to be taken on a return run to Brockenhurst. Two items are worth commenting on: first, the collection of fireman's irons and bits and pieces on the top of the side tank of the engine; and, second, the rural view of a country branch, with the single track following as far as possible the contours of the ground and the level crossing gates in the distance.

Today, the branch is still there, but not the pick-up goods nor the steam floating across the line.

' ... the coaling platform can be seen showing the implausibility of getting coal on the cab roof of the M7, No 30108.' Ex-Southern Railway Q Class 0-6-0, BR No 30535 shunting at Lymington Town – 27 November 1963.

'… shunting the small yard which operation required the locomotive and wagons to pass right through the shed.'
Ex-Southern Railway Q Class 0-6-0, BR No 30546 shunting at Lymington Town – 16 January 1964.

'… my presence on the footplate was tolerated on the strict understanding I did not step onto the driver's side of the cab … '
View from the cab of BR 2-6-2T, No 41224 – 26 February 1965.

HOLIDAY ISLAND IN THE SUN

The Isle of Wight used to be a fascinating place for the enthusiast, right up until the middle 1960s. As a result, a great deal of thought was necessary, not to decide which scenes to use but which ones to discard. From those that were eventually chosen, we start with a scene showing BR No W22 *Brading*, taken on 19 March 1966. This was an ex-L&SWR 0-4-4T of the 02 Class. At that time, all the steam locomotives remaining on the island were of the same class but did not make the interest any the less for that.

'Clean in its black and lined livery with polished brasswork ... ' BR 02 Class 0-4-4T No W22 *Brading*, at Ryde Esplanade on 19 March 1966, waiting to take the 13.28 to Ventnor.

Due to repair work on Ryde Pier at this time, trains were starting from Ryde Esplanade and this was the only time I am aware of actually using Ryde Esplanade station. Clean in its black and lined livery, with polished brasswork, *Brading* was waiting to take the 13.28 to Ventnor.

The next station along the line was Ryde St Johns. At this date, Ryde St Johns had taken over from Newport as the hub of railway activity on the Isle of Wight. It is difficult to appreciate the extent of the railway infrastructure that existed at Newport in the days when you could catch trains there, whence they left for all points of the compass. Here at St Johns on 16 September 1965, I have included an atmospheric view of W14 *Fishbourne* leaving with a train for Newport and Cowes. By walking a few

'... an atmospheric view ...' BR
02 Class 0-4-4T No W14
Fishbourne leaving Ryde St
Johns on 16 September 1965
with a train for Newport and
Cowes.

'... under a timber-framed hoist sits *Brading*...' BR 02 Class 0-4-4T No W22 *Brading* under repair outside Ryde St Johns works on 16 September 1965.

paces across the platform, it was possible to take an earlier view of W22 *Brading* than shown in the photograph used to start this section. Railways on the Isle of Wight were almost totally self-sufficient and at St Johns there existed a small works and repair shop. Here, under a timber-framed hoist, sits *Brading*, minus her coupling rods, receiving repair.

The final shot illustrating Ryde St Johns was taken on 19 March 1966 from the carriage of a train leaving for Ventnor. This shows a very necessary piece of investment carried out by the old Southern Railway who had built a new locomotive shed at St Johns. Even with creeping closure reducing the island's railways to a shadow of their former glory, the fixed plant has not been allowed to deteriorate. At this date, March 1966, the closure of the line beyond Shanklin was only a fortnight away and the last visit to Ventnor, by train, was being made. Ventnor was blessed with a most unusual seaside railway terminus. Set high above the town, the line from Wroxall arrived through the longest tunnel on the island. Driven under St Boniface Down, it extended to within a few yards of the platform ramps. The station and small goods yard were laid out within a tiny area, literally carved out of the chalk of the Down.

With the arrival of a passenger train, the engine would uncouple and run forward onto a head shunt. This was barely long enough for the locomotive and almost close enough to the pavement of the road immediately beyond for pedestrians to touch. With the points set for the outermost platform face, the locomotive could take water from an adjacent column. The photograph of No W29 *Alverstone* was taken on 16 September 1965 alongside the water column. In this scene, the set of the point under the locomotive wheels will take it away from the outside platform in order to round its train. So close is the entrance of the tunnel to the platforms, this manoeuvre will require the engine to run into the tunnel. The shot of W27 *Merstone*, shown here on 19 March 1966, was actually taken from the public thoroughfare outside the station. Only the most rudimentary of servicing

' ... necessary piece of investment carried out by the old Southern Railway ... ' Ryde St Johns' locomotive shed and signal box photographed from a Ventnor train on 19 March 1966.

'With the points set for the outermost platform face, the locomotive could take water from an adjacent column.' BR 02 Class 0-4-4T No. W29 *Alverstone* at Ventnor on 16 September 1965.

' ... the fireman has taken the opportunity to clear the smokebox of char.' BR 02 Class 0-4-4T No W27 *Merstone* at Ventnor on 19 March 1966.

facilities were provided and while the tanks are filled with water, the fireman has taken the opportunity to clear the smokebox of char – a filthy job, particularly on a windy day. The fine ash grit can be seen blowing back across the engine and fireman in this picture.

The last photograph in this section was taken on 19 September 1965 and shows W28 *Ashey* waiting to leave Ventnor with the six coaches forming the 16.42 to Ryde Pier Head. Take a final look at the close proximity of the tunnel portal to the station platforms, the manner by which the station area was carved out of the Down and the flowers which were a charming feature of this station, before leaving for Ryde and the mainland.

' ... the manner by which the station area was carved out of the Down and the flowers which were a charming feature of this station.' BR 02 Class 0-4-4T No W28 *Ashey* waiting to leave Ventnor on 19 September 1965, with the 16.42 to Ryde Pier Head.

Broad Swathe of the Midlands and Shires

OXFORD AS A RAILWAY CENTRE

Oxford in the days of the steam locomotive was, to my mind, the ideal railway centre. There are those who would set it aside because of the dominance of the Great Western and the almost complete standardisation of that company's locomotive fleet. However, in pre-nationalisation days it was possible to see locomotives from each of the big four companies on a daily basis. The LMS had its own station and locomotive shed alongside the Great Western station. The Southern ran regularly into the station, bringing trains for the north from the south coast

' ... the Southern Region still handled their quota of south to north cross-country services.' Ex-Southern Railway original West Country 4-6-2 Pacific, BR No 34102 *Lapford* at Oxford on southbound *Pines Express* – 18 October 1963.

' ... running light on the through lines having come off shed ... '
Ex-Southern Railway, rebuilt West Country 4-6-2 Pacific, BR No 34024 *Tamar Valley* at Oxford – 2 April 1965.

and taking their counterparts from the north down to the south coast. And the LNER – well they came off the Great Central line through Banbury and could be seen as deep into Great Western country as Swindon.

By the 1960s, the LMS shed and station had been closed and passenger trains of the ex-LMS Bletchley line were dieselised. The through-passenger workings to the north were monopolised by ex-GWR locomotives but freight workings seemed to be just as frequent as they had even been and the Southern Region still handled their quota of south to north cross-country services. It is with the southbound expresses that I have chosen to start the illustrations for this section. Seen here on the southbound *Pines Express*, on 18 October 1963, is ex-Southern Railway original West Country 4-6-2 Pacific, BR No 34102 *Lapford*. This engine will have come up from its home shed, Bournemouth, with either the corresponding *Pines Express* or the Bournemouth-York. The Bournemouth-York cross-country run through Oxford was a long established train from before World War Two. The *Pines Express* which ran between Bournemouth and Manchester had, until the year before, taken a totally different route via Bath and the old Somerset & Dorset line to the south coast. The closure of the S&DR route in 1962 resulted in the *Pines Express* being routed via Oxford the following year. Turned out by Bournemouth shed in almost tip-top condition, *Lapford* was typical of the steam power to be seen at the time.

From an original West Country to a rebuilt version. The date was some eighteen months later, 2 April 1965, when there is a shot of a rebuilt West Country 4-6-2 Pacific, BR No 34024, *Tamar Valley*. We see this locomotive running light on through lines having come off shed in order to take over the southbound *Pines Express*. Today, when this picture is

'The smoke rising from the chimney indicates that the blower was working and the safety valves are lifted ... ' Ex-Southern Railway, rebuilt West Country 4-6-2 Pacific, BR No 34024 *Tamar Valley* at the head of the southbound *Pines Express* at Oxford – 2 April 1965.

compared with the previous one, it is hard to appreciate that the cost of rebuilding these locomotives just a few years before could be as little as between £8,000 and £11,000 a locomotive. Furthermore, for £11,000 the locomotive concerned was fitted with a new set of frames.

With the arrival of the southbound *Pines*, there would be a very smart change of engines and the new view is of *Tamar Valley* coupled to the train. The smoke rising from the chimney indicates that the blower was working and the safety valves are lifted and the boiler is blowing off. The fact that one of the crew is off the footplate and his mate is leaning out of the cab indicates that perhaps all is not well. Twenty-five years after the events of the early 1960s, those not being of an age to have actually followed the railway scene of the time can be forgiven for imagining that it was all grime and dirt. Yes, a great proportion of the locomotive stock created that impression, but generally speaking, and as can be seen elsewhere in this book, the coaching stock was kept fairly clean. I know that it was a beautiful sunny day when this picture was taken, but those coaches positively glisten.

Oxford was not only a railway centre and a junction of a number of lines, the city also had a large industrial base. As I mentioned earlier, there was a constant parade of freight trains through the station. The first of those shown depicts ex-GWR Prairie 61XX 2-6-2T, No 6156 on a down goods on 16 July 1963. This class of locomotive consisted of seventy engines all built in the early 1930s. They were built specifically to work the accelerated London suburban services, and the entire class was allocated to the London Division. The RCTS series *The Locomotives of The Great Western Railway* records, in a volume published in 1962, that this class of locomotive worked comparatively few goods trains. However, by the date of this photograph, it would appear that Oxford shed used them extensively for freight trains and from my own observations at this period, they exclusively worked the freight on the Thame branch. In the background to No 6156 can be seen the old London & North Western and subsequently the LMS Oxford locomotive shed. Closed in December 1950, it was still standing some 12 ½ years later.

' ... there was a constant parade of freight trains through the station.'
Ex-GWR Prairie 61XX Class 2-6-2T, No 6156 at Oxford – 16 July 1963.

' ... a wartime baby, built in 1943 ... '
Ex-GWR Hall Class 4-6-0, No 6952 *Kimberley Hall* at Oxford on a down freight – 18 October 1963.

The next freight shown is in an identical position and headed by an ex-GWR Hall Class 4-6-0, No 6952 *Kimberley Hall* on 18 October 1963. Although a wartime baby, built in 1943, somewhere along the line this engine had acquired a flat-sided Hawkesworth tender which was first introduced with his County Class 4-6-0 in 1945. What a difference a sunny day makes to the scene, bringing out the colours of the lower quadrant signal gantry!

Going back in time again to 16 July 1963, I have included a picture of another down freight headed by ex-GWR 38XX Class 2-8-0 No 3845. This was the Great Western Railway's classic freight engine which ran very freely. Notwithstanding that, the approach to Oxford station in the down direction was up a 1 in 150 gradient – my notes record that this locomotive was 'flat out'. It must have been something for a special note to have been made, but even so the fireman has found time to lean out of the cab to have his photograph taken. Also worthy of note is the background, clean coaches of course and two of the ubiquitous railway spotters of the era to keep me company. I wonder will they see and recognise themselves after all these years?

The last of the quartet of freights shown is again travelling in the down direction. The date is again that sunny day of 18 October 1963, and the locomotive is a British Rail standard Britannia Class 4-6-2 Pacific, No 70028 *Royal Star*. She is seen here accelerating up that 1 in 150 into the station with a train of flats loaded up with cars – another of my favourite photographs.

From down freight trains to down passenger trains and the Bournemouth-York train after the Western Region had taken over from Southern Region motive power. Taken on 2 April 1965, the first photograph shows a rather sad looking ex-GWR 68XX Grange Class 4-6-0, No 6841

' ... the fireman has found time to lean out of the cab to have his photograph taken.'
Ex-GWR 38XX Class 2-8-0, No 3845 on down freight at Oxford – 16 July 1963.

'... accelerating up that 1 in 150 into the station with a train of flats loaded up with cars ... ' British Rail Standard Britannia Class 4-6-2 Pacific, No 70028 *Royal Star* with a down freight at Oxford – 18 October 1963.

Marlas Grange minus name and number plates. The Grange Class of the GWR family of standard 4-6-0 locomotives was very much the poor relation. It was overshadowed by the more glamorous Hall Class with which its locomotives shared like duties. However, they were, I understood from various operating staff, a much stronger locomotive than those of the Hall Class. This statement appears to be borne out by the fact that you saw Grange Class locomotives regularly to the end of steam but not Hall Class locomotives. It is curious that no Grange Class locomotive has been preserved, or were they all driven into the ground in the last few months?

I close the page on Oxford station with another view of the Bournemouth-York waiting to leave on 18 October 1963. This time the motive power is immaculate in the form of ex-GWR Modified Hall Class 4-6-0, No 6960 *Raveningham Hall*. More than 26 years after this photograph was taken it was reproduced in the magazine *Model Railways*. Following its reproduction, I was approached by a fellow member of the Gauge O Guild who advised me that the fireman complimenting the spotless condition of the locomotive was his driver at work. On the demise of steam and consequent dieselisation of motive power, Fireman John Broughton, as I learnt his name was, had left British Rail. Small world that this is, the publication of his picture all those years later resulted in my being able to send him a personalised copy of his own.

' ... they were, I understood from various operating staff, a muoh stronger looomotivo than those of the Hall Class.'
Ex-GWR 68XX Grange Class 4-6-0, No 6841 *Marlas Grange* at the head of the Bournemouth-York, leaving Oxford – 2 April 1965.

'This time the motive power is immaculate ... '
Ex-GWR Modified Hall Class 4-6-0, No 6960 *Raveningham Hall* at the head of the Bournemouth-York at Oxford – 18 October 1963.

ON SHED – GREAT WESTERN STYLE

From Oxford station to the old Great Western Railway shed at Oxford. By the date of my visit on 16 May 1965, the shed was in a state of terminal decay. In fact, I cannot believe that the structure was safe. The shed itself dated from 1854 and was built to accommodate both broad and standard gauge engines. Over the years, the offices and store were rebuilt, a steel-framed repair shed was added and a standard GWR coaling stage was added during World War Two. The engine shed just got patched and repaired and survived until closure in January 1967.

The shed had four roads and the photograph shows ex-GWR 61XX

' ... I cannot believe that the structure was safe. The shed itself dated from 1854 ... '
Ex-GWR 61XX Class 2-6-2T, No 6154 in Oxford locomotive shed – 16 May 1965.

Class 2-6-2T, No 6154 in the left-hand one of the two centre roads. The road with the BR Standard locomotive showing had a ridge vent in the roof to the single road. The other three roads sufficed with a ridge vent over the road to the right of No 6154 in the centre of the picture. Everything was built in timber – even the columns were in timber – and the roof was slated. To have survived for 113 years is, I suppose, a tribute to those who designed and built it in the first place. It is also a wonder that it never burned down.

The tank engine which, I imagine, most people associate with the Great Western is the 0-6-0 Pannier tank. Pannier tanks came in a variety of sizes but all, when viewed from the front, had a waddling gait while running. The most common of their number were those of the 57XX Class. Just for the record, because they do not feature elsewhere in this book, I have included a view of No 3751, which was also on Oxford shed that day.

'Pannier tanks came in a variety of sizes … '
Ex-GWR 57XX Class 0-6-0PT, No 3751 at Oxford locomotive shed – 16 May 1965.

' ... would have worked an inter-region service into Oxford.'
BR Standard Class 5 4-6-0, No 73083 at Oxford locomotive shed – 16 May 1965.

The visit was made on a Sunday and locomotives were standing on all the yard roads. Among these was a BR Standard Class 5, 4-6-0, No 73083 carrying Southern discs on the lamp irons. This was one of the BR Standard Class 5 locomotives allocated to the Southern Region and would have worked an inter-region service into Oxford. When the old Southern Railways King Arthur Class were withdrawn, the names were transferred to the BR Standard Class 5 locomotives allocated to the Southern Region. At one time, No 73083 had acquired the name *Pendragon* but by this time the name plate had found another home.

Typical of the locomotives to be found on most ex-Great Western sheds were the two further types photographed at Oxford on 16 May 1965. The first is one of the ex-GWR 38XX Class 2-8-0 freight locomotives, No 3854, selected because, despite its rust streaked smokebox, the classic GWR lines come over well. Despite this locomotive's appearance and that of those others in view, it should be remembered that Oxford was still very much a busy working depot and all the engines in view would have rostered duties the next day.

Before leaving Oxford for a second GWR locomotive shed, another look at ex-GWR Grange Class 4-6-0, No 6841 *Marlas Grange*. This was shown earlier in the section on Oxford station, waiting to leave with the Bournemouth-York. That photograph, taken six weeks earlier, shows the left-hand side of the engine and both the name and number plates had been removed. On this, the right-hand side, only the name plate had been

'Typical of the locomotives to be found on most ex-Great Western sheds ... '
Ex-GWR 38XX 2-8-0, No 3854 at Oxford locomotive shed – 16 May 1965.

'At this time Swindon were selling cab sideplates at £4.00 a time and Hall Class name plates for £17.00 a throw.'
Ex-GWR Grange Class 4-6-0, No 6841 *Marlas Grange* at Oxford locomotive shed – 16 May 1965.

'... the container-like building was the repair shop, another wartime addition.'
General view of Banbury locomotive depot – 4 March 1967.

removed leaving the number plate still there. At this time Swindon was selling cab sideplates at £4.00 a time and Hall Class name plates for £17.00 a throw. If only I knew then what I know now!

From Oxford shed to its neighbour at Banbury. In Great Western days, Banbury, with nearly 80 locomotives allocated, had nearly half as many again as Oxford. It was also blessed with much more room and a basic shed that was fifty plus years younger. The general view was taken on 4 March 1967, shortly after the shed closure, although all the facilities for servicing steam locomotives were still available. Starting from the right, the ramp leads to a coaling stage. The roofless walls were all that was left of an ash shelter provided during the war. No doubt this was an attempt to maintain the blackout for locomotives dropping or clearing out the firebox. Still to the left again, there is the shed building proper, a four-road straight shed. Next to the shed were three dead-end roads, used for both storage of locomotives and the breakdown or work train. Last of all, the container-like building was the repair shop, another wartime addition.

Turning the clock back a little to the wet Sunday morning of 16 May

1965. The next scene is taken from the entrance of the repair shop. The locomotive on the left is BR Standard 9F 2-10-0, No 92073. It is only when seen from this angle that the true impact of the size of the tenders attached to the 9Fs is apparent. The locomotive directly in front of the camera is ex-GWR Grange Class 4-6-0, No 6853 *Morehampton Grange* and the collection of modeller's bits and pieces between the Grange and the camera came off an ex-GWR 56XX 0-6-2T under repair in the lifting shop. From the repair shop, I walked over to the left where I climbed onto the footplate of a locomotive standing on the middle of the three dead-end roads. This enabled me to record an ex-GWR 56XX 0-6-2T, No 6697 and part of the standby breakdown and tool train. The latter provided a splash of colour to a very bleak morning. The shed, from this view, can also be seen to be in a far better condition than that with which the Oxford men had to contend. At the front of the shed was another ex-GWR Grange Class 4-6-0, No 6866 *Morfa Grange*. Like all its sister members in the Grange Class at the time, it too was minus name and number plates.

   From the front of the shed, a turn down the other side where, beyond

' ... the collection of modeller's bits and pieces, between the Grange and the camera came off an ex-GWR 56XX 0-6-2T under repair in the lifting shop.' BR Standard 9F 2-10-0 freight locomotive No 92073 and ex-GWR Grange Class 4-6-0, No 6853 *Morehampton Grange* at Banbury locomotive shed – 16 May 1965.

' ... and part of the standby breakdown and tool train.'
Ex-GWR 56XX Class 0-6-2T, No 6697 at Banbury locomotive shed – 16 May 1965.

'Like all its sister members in the Grange Class at the time, it too was minus name and number plates.'
Ex-GWR Grange Class 4-6-0, No 6866 *Morfa Grange* at Banbury locomotive shed – 16 May 1965.

'... with every possible piece of brasswork polished and re-polished.'
BR-built GWR Castle Class 4-6-0, No 7029 *Clun Castle* at Banbury locomotive shed – 4 March 1967.

'Just looking at her makes my back ache!'
BR-built GWR Castle Class 4-6-0, No 7029 *Clun Castle* at Banbury locomotive shed – 4 March 1967.

the ash shelter seen in the general view of the shed, there was the turntable. Using the turntable in preparation for a special to Birkenhead, on 4 March 1967, was BR built GWR Castle Class 4-6-0, No 7029 *Clun Castle*. She was prepared with every possible piece of brasswork polished and re-polished. Curiously, for such an event, other than the BR staff from the shed, there were probably no more than half a dozen people watching the preparations. Steam was already a memory at Banbury and I leave you with a comment I overhead from one ex-fireman to his mate – "Just looking at her makes my back ache!"

INDUSTRIAL SADDLE TANK LOCOMOTIVES

To me there has always been a more friendly and approachable air to the industrial locomotive. They were built in their thousands by the private locomotive manufacturers who each stamped their products with discernible characteristics. They used to be seen in tantalising glimpses, perhaps over the top of a line of coal wagons or disappearing around the corner of a warehouse, before you had time to take in what it was or to whom it belonged. Today, many a preserved line relies heavily on ex-industrial locomotives which had never hauled a passenger train until acquired for preservation.

This section is given over to the industrial locomotive in its working habitat. A selection of eight scenes showing seven different locomotives. Two characteristics are common to all seven locomotives. First, each locomotive

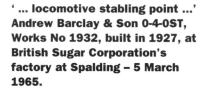

' ... locomotive stabling point ...'
Andrew Barclay & Son 0-4-0ST,
Works No 1932, built in 1927, at
British Sugar Corporation's
factory at Spalding – 5 March
1965.

' ... the all-round visibility cab of many an industrial locomotive.' Andrew Barclay & Son 0-4-0ST, Works No 1931, built in 1927, at British Sugar Corporation's factory – 3 February 1966.

has a saddle tank – a type of design that had been almost totally abandoned by British Railways after grouping, the saddle tank lasted until the very end for the industrial steam locomotive. The second feature is that none of those shown are painted black. Unlike British Rail where black painted engines were the basic rule, with industrial locomotives it was the exception. The only black painted industrial locomotive I photographed was one belonging to the National Coal Board. Unique as that particular locomotive was, in that it was a rebuilt Austerity with an underfeed stoker and gas producer combustion system, this section will stay with those painted in colour.

The first two scenes could, at first glance, easily be mistaken for the same locomotive. Both scenes are at the same place, the locomotive stabling point at the British Sugar Corporation factory at Spalding. The locomotive in the first picture can be identified accurately. It is an Andrew Barclay & Son 0-4-0ST, Works No 1932, built in 1927 and photographed on 5 March 1965. When compared with its twin sister in the next picture, all sorts of modifications are apparent. The second photograph, showing BSC No 2 was also taken at Spalding but nearly a year later on 3 February 1966. Again it is an Andrew Barclay & Son 0-4-0ST, Works No 1931 and was also built in 1927. The photograph of BSC No 2 shows what can best be described as the all-round visibility cab of many an industrial locomotive. On the other hand, the chunky workmanlike appearance comes across well in the view from this angle.

From Spalding, a lengthy cross-country journey in a south-westerly direction would bring you to Byfield. Byfield used to be on the old Stratford-upon-Avon and Midland Junction Railway, a little west of its junction with the Great Central at Woodford. There, on 24 April 1965, you would have found an 0-6-0ST *No 3 Avonside*, built by Avonside in 1924, Works No 1919 and painted in a deep Prussian blue. This locomotive is not standing in a farmer's field but on a private line leading to Stewarts & Lloyds iron ore quarries and possibly no more than 100 yards away from the S&MJR main line. Shortly after this photograph was taken, this locomotive was transferred to the owner's Cranford quarries and subsequently preserved on the Foxfield Light Railway, Dilhorne, Staffs.

Keeping *No 3 Avonside* company that day was another 0-6-0ST *Cherwell*. This was built by W G Bagnall in 1942, Works No 2654. Subsequent to this photograph, *Cherwell* found another 'home' in the New Street Recreation Playground, Daventry, but in what condition I know not.

From Byfield, another cross-country journey, not as far as previously, this time in a south-easterly direction to Dunstable. Here, in steam at the APCM Houghton Regis Works, on 8 June 1965, I discovered an Andrew Barclay & Son 0-4-0ST. Carrying the name *Punch Hull* and a plate recording the fact that she had been rebuilt by P Baker & Co. of Cardiff in 1928, she is the oldest of the industrial locomotives illustrated. Life for

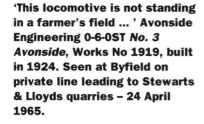

'This locomotive is not standing in a farmer's field ... ' Avonside Engineering 0-6-0ST *No. 3 Avonside*, Works No 1919, built in 1924. Seen at Byfield on private line leading to Stewarts & Lloyds quarries – 24 April 1965.

'Keeping *No. 3 Avonside* company that day, was another 0-6-0ST, *Cherwell*.' W G Bagnall 0-6-0ST *Cherwell*, Works No 2654, built in 1942. Seen at Byfield on private line leading to Stewarts & Lloyds quarries – 24 April 1965.

' ... one of my favourite photographs.' Andrew Barclay & Son 0-4-0ST, *Punch Hull*, Works No 776, built 1896 at APCM Works Houghton Regis – 8 June 1965.

Punch Hull started in 1896 as Andrew Barclay Works No 776 and continues today at the Buckinghamshire Railway Centre, Quainton – definitely one of my favourite photographs.

We now travel from Dunstable east to Felsted in Essex to see another British Sugar Corporation locomotive. Here, on 14 June 1966, I photographed another of their 0-4-0STs. My records do no more than state the date of the photograph, but it has all the appearance of the same batch from Andrew Barclay as the first two locomotives illustrating this section. By June 1966, this factory no longer received any sugar beet by rail and had converted to oil firing. The extensive sidings which should have been in the background had been lifted and the engine itself was awaiting disposal.

The last two scenes in this section are both of the same engine, another from British Sugar Corporation's stock. Both photographs were taken at Bardney in Lincolnshire on 12 July 1966 and show Hudswell Clarke 0-6-0ST, Works No 1604, at the end of the line. Despite its 'antique' appearance, this locomotive was built as late as 1928. These two scenes show how frugal were the facilities that were provided for the maintenance and operation of the industrial locomotive. Unlike the railway companies where the locomotive stock was an end in itself, industry saw them as another tool and only the means to achieve an altogether different end. However, Bardney was not the end for this example from the Hudswell Clarke stable as it found a new home at the Kirton Lindsay Windmill and Museum in Lincolnshire.

'... and the engine itself was awaiting disposal.' Andrew Barclay & Son 0-4-0ST at British Sugar Corporation's factory – 14 June 1966.

' ... how frugal were the facilities that were provided for the maintenance and operation of the industrial locomotive.' Hudswell Clarke 0-6-0ST, Works No 1604, built 1928, shown at British Sugar Corporation's factory, Bardney – 12 July 1966.

'Despite its 'antique' appearance, this locomotive was built as late as 1928.' Hudswell Clarke 0-6-0ST, Works No 1604, built 1928, shown at British Sugar Corporation's factory, Bardney – 12 July 1966.

POT-POURRI

Pot-pourri – a literary medley or, in this case, a selection of illustrations which do not fall comfortably into any of the groupings selected. I have started with an illustration which stretches the concept of Midlands and Shires, but Salisbury is in Wiltshire, and comfortably gets us in the general direction taken by the following sections.

The date was 30 April 1964 and the locomotive an ex-Southern Railway original West Country Class Pacific 4-6-2, BR No 34038 *Lynton*, leaving with the 5.15 pm semi-fast for Waterloo, arriving at 7.49 pm having stopped at Andover, Basingstoke, Woking and Surbiton on the way. This gave an overall average 'schedule' speed of just under 32 mph. For a

' ... while pulling away from Salisbury, I would imagine that this turn was one that should not have taxed the fireman that day.'
Ex-Southern Railway original West Country Class Pacific 4-6-2, BR No 34038 *Lynton* leaving Salisbury with the 5.15pm semi-fast to London – 30 April 1964.

locomotive in as good a condition as *Lynton* appeared to be while pulling away from Salisbury, I would imagine that this turn was one that should not have taxed the fireman that day.

Following *Lynton* up to Basingstoke and joining the old Great Western branch brings us to Reading. A visit there on 8 November 1963 found me having difficulties in lining up the locomotives with suitable light. However, I have selected two shots illustrating locomotives which would not otherwise have been included. The first shown at Reading is ex-GWR Manor Class 4-6-0, No 7817 *Garsington Manor*. For most of my time at Reading that day, *Garsington Manor* sat in one of the bay platforms at the east end of the station, effectively obscured for photographic purposes by the platform canopy. From this rear view, as the engine left the bay, it can be seen that the crew have just let the tarpaulin protection hang down from the cab roof, instead of attaching it to the bracket on the tender provided for that purpose. This would be fine while doing a little light shunting around the station, but I wonder what the crew would have done if the station foreman had told them to hand 7817 over to the crew of a disabled engine on an up-express to Paddington.

A move to the west end of Reading station brought me a slice of luck in the form of an ex-GWR 47XX Class 2-8-0. The example shown is No 4706 coasting through the station on a down-goods so quietly that she nearly passed without me realising until too late to photograph. The 47XX Class only consisted of nine engines and no doubt survived because of the GWR

' ... as the engine left the bay, it can be seen that the crew have just let the tarpaulin protection hang down from the cab roof ... '
Ex-GWR Manor Class 4-6-0, No 7817 *Garsington Manor* at the east end of Reading (General) – 8 November 1963.

policy of standardisation. They were large engines exceeded in weight on the GWR only by the King Class locomotives. Although occasionally used on passenger duties, they were very much the kings of freight locomotives and the green livery was appropriate.

Moving from Reading to the north-west of Oxford and the old LMS route between Oxford and Bletchley, I chanced on a piece of railway operation that no longer exists. The illustration shows a gated crossing a few miles north-east of Islip. The locomotive is an ex-LMS Class 5, 4-6-0, BR No 45299, with an unfitted freight train. Although the line was clear, the train came to a halt by the crossing keeper's house. The crossing keeper appeared, he with the frown on his face, and went to see the locomotive crew. After a while the train started and went on its way to Bletchley leaving behind two or three highly polished churns of the type seen outside gypsy caravans for storing water.

I did not get the chance to establish whether this was actually the case because 'he with the frown on his face' came and remonstrated with me for being on the wrong side of the railway fence. Pointing out that the crossing was there for that purpose only created more stubbornness, so I returned to my car and went on my way never since having had an opportunity to return.

Follow the old Great Western line from Oxford far enough west and you will come to Hereford where, on 16 May 1964, I found an ex-GWR Grange Class 4-6-0, No 6850 *Cleeve Grange*. At the head of a cross-country freight, *Cleeve Grange* was taking water from a column alongside the goods avoiding line to the station. Freight trains had regular halts such as this,

'Although the line was clear, the train came to a halt by the crossing keeper's house.'
Ex-LMS Class 5, 4-6-0, BR No 45299 at a level crossing just north-east of Islip on the Oxford-Bletchley line – 4 February 1964.

' ... taking water from a column alongside the goods avoiding line ...'
Ex-GWR Grange Class 4-6-0, No 6850 *Cleeve Grange* at Hereford – 16 May 1964.

'Their appearance was greeted by almost universal dismay ... '
Ex-LMS Ivatt 2-6-0, BR No 43007 at Madeley Road – 18 July 1967.

where the driver and fireman would top the tender up with water, pull the fire round, check the moving parts and wait for the passenger trains to clear the road in front. When they got the signal to continue down the line, it would be no time at all before they were replaced by the next freight and the routine would be repeated.

Away from Hereford, in search of another class of locomotive, we travel north-east across country to the old North Staffordshire Railway's branch to Market Drayton. There, on the site of the old Madeley Road station on 18 July 1967. I came across an ex-LMS 2-6-0, BR No 43007. These locomotives were introduced, post-war, by Ivatt of the LMS. Their appearance was greeted by almost universal dismay on the part of the railway cogniscenti, an opinion which I still share.

From Madeley Road, which only saw the freight handling traffic to and from Madeley Colliery, we travel again in a north-easterly direction to a railway centre of great importance, Doncaster, on a very foggy morning. On 24 January 1966, I was travelling to York on the 9.00am from Kings Cross and while my train was standing in Doncaster station, ex-LNER-V2 Class 2-6-2, BR No 60886 slowly passed and stopped a little way down the line. Out came the camera and as my train drew out of the station, I took a chance exposure. The result is all steam, smoke and fog, but the classic lines of a Gresley engine are unmistakable.

' ... as my train drew out of the station, I took a chance exposure.'
Ex-LNER V2 Class 2-6-2, BR No 60886 at Doncaster – 24 January 1966.

STOP-OVER ON THE LICKEY INCLINE

Over the years, the Lickey Incline became well known, not only within the circle of railway enthusiasts but also to the travelling public generally. There were a number of reasons for this awareness. The Lickey was on the old Midland main line between Bristol and Birmingham which carried a dense and heavy service of both freight and passengers. The incline itself was a major operating obstacle throughout the period of steam haulage. Two miles of incline at 1 in 37 starting at Bromsgrove and climbing to Blackwell, represent problems not just for trains ascending but also for those descending. Another reason was the publicity given to the Midland Railway's 0-10-0 locomotive, built specially for banking up the incline and christened 'Big Bertha'. The LNER built a much larger and more powerful

'... waiting for its next tour of duty at Bromsgrove.'
GWR-designed BR 84XX 0-6-OPT, No 8400 at Bromsgrove - 29 February 1964.

Garrett locomotive for banking freight trains at Wath on the old Great Central, but the ex-Midland Decapod was the engine that kept itself in the public eye.

I had to make a special trip to cover the Lickey and this was finally achieved by visiting a friend and colleague who lived in Bromsgrove. By early 1964 there were all sorts of rumours as to how long steam would continue banking the incline and my visit was not made at a time conducive to striking photographic results. Even worse than had been feared met me when I arose on 29 February 1964 - thick fog. This was very slow to clear and in scenes shot during the morning it is difficult to distinguish where the fog ends and the steam and smoke starts!

By the date of my visit, the old Midland influence which had lasted throughout the LMS period, had disappeared. 'Big Bertha', the unique 0-10-0 locomotive, had been replaced by a frequently seen locomotive class in the form of a BR Standard 9F Class 2-10-0. The clutch of Midland 3F Class 0-6-0T locomotives had been replaced by GWR-designed pannier tanks built for BR by Bagnall after nationalisation. One of these pannier tanks, BR No 8400 is shown in the first photograph. Seen here it is waiting for its next turn of duty at Bromsgrove. Locomotives waited on standby a few hundred yards south of the station at a small servicing point. Walking back over the access bridge, I took a shot of the BR Standard 9F Class 2-10-0 freight locomotive No 92230 which had been waiting behind the pannier tank.

By that time the pannier had moved off for another banking duty. The view of the 9F 2-10-0 from above shows that, although it is February,

'... although it is February, the cab roof ventilator has been opened.'
BR Standard 9F Class 2-10-0 freight locomotive No 92230 at Bromsgrove - 29 February 1964.

the cab roof ventilator has been opened. There are also signs of a more important item in the form of sand for the driving wheels. This can be seen where it has been spilt on the footplate along the boiler while topping up the sand boxes.

As the day wore on the fog slowly lifted and the afternoon was spent on the incline, but it was still a dull, drab day. Typical of the scenes that day is that shown of a freight ascending the incline headed by an ex-LMS 8F Class 2-8-0, BR No 48629. Working to its limit, only the locomotive was visible as the moving cloud of smoke and steam that it produced totally obscured the train following.

Descending the hill by freight trains was almost as problematical as for trains in the other direction. Granted they did not need a banker, but loose-fitted freight trains had their brakes pinned down to the extent that locomotives had to haul their trains down the incline. Running down the incline is ex-LMS 4F 0-6-0, BR No 44580. This locomotive was hauling one of those variegated freight trains, made up of dozens of different types of wagons, which made the observation of freight trains so interesting.

At the top of the incline was Blackwell where it eased to a mere 1 in 291 but continued almost to Barnt Green, 1 ½ miles towards Birmingham. Barnt Green was the junction for the lengthy loop line via Redditch and Evesham avoiding the Lickey Incline. Although only meeting the needs of an area with a very small, village-sized populous, it was served with nearly thirty trains a day stopping in each direction. The station was quite enormous and clearly one of those white elephants acquired by British Rail which ran up the initial losses of the 1950s. It was obviously included in the

'... only the locomotive was visible as the moving cloud of smoke and steam that it produced totally obscured the train following.'
Ex-LMS 8F Class 2-8-0, BR No 48629 climbing Lickey Incline at the head of a freight train - 29 February 1964.

'... loose-fitted freight trains had their brakes pinned down to the extent that locomotives had to haul their trains down the incline.'
Ex-LMS 4F 0-6-0, BR No 44580 descending Lickey Incline - 29 February 1964.

'The station was quite enormous and clearly one of those white elephants acquired by British Rail...'
Ex-LMS Jubilee Class 4-6-0, BR No 45674 *Duncan* running through Barnt Green station with a Bristol-bound freight - 29 February 1964.

itinerary for the day and while there a Bristol-bound fitted freight came through, headed by an ex-LMS Jubilee Class 4-6-0, BR No 45674 *Duncan*. The freshly painted smokebox prompted a fellow enthusiast to comment on seeing the photograph that 'it must have come out of Saltley'. Saltley was the huge ex-Midland, and subsequently LMS, engine shed in Birmingham. Observation which gave rise to the conclusion made in that quoted comment ensured that the enthusiast who was aware was never bored.

To BIRKENHEAD BY SPECIAL

As far as possible, I have avoided using too many shots obviously taken of, or from, enthusiasts' specials. To do so could easily create a balance which does not reflect the day-to-day scenes during the steam era. On the other hand, there were a considerable number of enthusiasts' specials over those years and they were a part of the railway scene. They provided opportunities to travel over many lines which no longer had a passenger service or, as in the case of one section in this book, a line which, to my knowledge, had never had a passenger service. In addition, the locomotives were generally, but not always, turned out in first class external appearance - a positive advantage with colour film. I have, however, tried to avoid showing locomotives which had already been preserved, although any number shown in these pages were subsequently rescued from the scrap heap.

'... *Pendennis Castle*' has since travelled rather farther than she did that day as this locomotive is now 'down-under' in Australia.'
Ex-GWR Castle Class 4-6-0, No 4079 *Pendennis Castle* leaving Banbury with a special to Birkenhead - 4 March 1967.

'... the station pilot was given the full treatment and kept as a showpiece.' Ex-LMS 4P 2-6-4T, BR No 42616 at Birkenhead (Woodside) - 5 March 1967.

I believe I am correct in saying from this distance in time, that only two of the locomotives that appear in these pages had already achieved preservation status. One of these is shown in the first photograph. It is an ex-GWR Castle Class 4-6-0, No 4079 *Pendennis Castle* shown leaving Banbury with a special to Birkenhead (Woodside) on Saturday, 4 March 1967. During the course of that weekend there were to be no less than four specials to Birkenhead (Woodside). The reason for this interest was the completion of a further stage of the electrification on the West Coast main line out of Euston. This resulted in the express services out of Paddington, on the old Great Western route through Birmingham (Snow Hill), to Birkenhead being withdrawn. *Pendennis Castle* has since travelled rather farther than she did that day as this locomotive is now 'down-under' in Australia.

The next day the Stephenson Locomotive Society organised two special trains to run a return trip from Birmingham (Tyseley) to Birkenhead (Woodside). The following illustration shows ex-LMS Stanier 2-6-4T, BR No 42616, acting as station pilot at Birkenhead on 5 March 1967. In LMS days these locomotives were given a 4P classification which was revised by British Rail to 4MT, more appropriate to its duties by that date. Often, as seen here, the station pilot was given the full treatment and kept as a showpiece. In this instance it is framed by typical terminal station architecture.

Another showpiece locomotive that day was the BR Standard 9F 2-10-0 freight locomotive No 92234. This locomotive replaced ex-GWR Castle *Clun Castle* at Chester for the run to Birkenhead and back to Chester. I have used a small sequence showing No 92234 because in the right circumstances and conditions, it could be shown as a very striking and impressive locomotive.

Starting at Woodside, No 92234 is being coupled back onto the special for the return to Chester. The station throat was laid in a tunnel which started immediately off the end of the platform ramps and I stood under the tunnel portal in order to take that photograph. On starting, trains had a stiff climb up through the tunnel to join the four-track main line across Wirral. The SLS tours always used to include a number of photographic stops which were obviously chosen with care. One of these that day was at Hooton on the Wirral and the afternoon sun shows to the full the powerful face of the Standard 9F freight locomotive. On arrival at Chester the 9F 2-10-0 came off the train and was replaced for the return to Tyseley by a Class 5 4-6-0. Before the 9F came off the train, I took a final shot at Chester looking down the right-hand side of the engine. This shows a couple of items of interest in retrospect. The first is the old London & North Western signal box seen beyond the smoke deflector of the 9F. A visitor today cannot have any comprehension of the size of the traffic that passed through Chester every day, or the scope of the facilities required in order

'... No 92234 is being coupled back onto the special for the return to Chester.'
BR Standard 9F 2-10-0 freight locomotive being coupled to SLS special at Birkenhead (Woodside) - 5 March 1967.

'... the afternoon sun shows to the full the powerful face of the Standard 9F freight locomotive.'
BR Standard 9F 2-10-0 freight locomotive at Hooton (Wirral) with SLS special - 5 March 1967.

'... a coloured circle. This was the old GWR classification system for route availability ...'
BR Standard 9F 2-10-0 freight locomotive at Chester with SLS special - 5 March 1967.

'... a typical station scene of the steam era - the covered footbridge, the cattle pens behind the locomotive...'
BR Class 5 4-6-0, No 44680 at Ruabon with an SLS special - 5 March 1967.

that it could be handled. The signal box shown here was only one of several necessary for the traffic. The second is another of those pre-nationalisation operating practices which continued in the respective regions for many years. Seen on the cab side of the 9F is a coloured circle. This was the old GWR classification system for route availability for different locomotive classes and was handed down to BR standard locomotives on the Western Region.

Before closing on the rites held that weekend over the Great Western route, a shot taken at Ruabon on the return journey. The special I was travelling on was hauled back to Tyseley by Class 5 4-6-0, No 44680. A photograph stop at Ruabon recorded a typical station scene of the steam era - the covered footbridge, the cattle pens behind the locomotive and enough smoke and steam to give it movement and life.

CROMFORD AND HIGH PEAK

The Cromford and High Peak was never a regular haunt of the enthusiast, even though its claim to the record books was beyond challenge. The entry in the record books would show that the line included Hopton Incline which, with a gradient of 1 in 14, was operated by steam locomotives right up to closure in April 1967. The line was freight only, remote and inaccessible, particularly when private car ownership was a fraction of that today. The scenes shown were all taken on 30 April 1967 when three brake van specials ran over sections of the line. These, I believe, were the last revenue earning trains to run over the line between Middleton Top and Parsley Hay. Middleton Top was near the eastern end of the line, set between the villages of Middleton and Wirksworth and some 8 or 10 miles north of Derby. Middleton Top is at the top of cable-operated inclines which led down to Cromford Wharf. I say 'is' because the winding house

'... arrived empty at Middleton Top ...'
BR J94 0-6-0STs, Nos 68006 and 68012 arrive at Middleton Top with six brake vans to form SLS special to Parsley Hay and return. In the background, behind the water tank can be seen the remains of the roofless, single road engine shed and the pyramidal roof and tall chimney, housing the beam engine at the top of the incline down to Sheep Pasture - 30 April 1967.

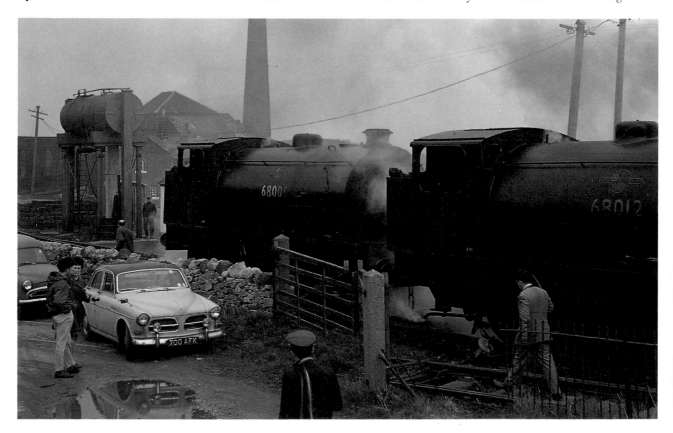

'... an unusual 'water tower' which appears to have been constructed from a life-expired Lancashire boiler.'
BR J94 0-6-0STs, Nos 68006 and 68012 take water at Middleton Top - 30 April 1967.

'... and run round the train.'
BR J94 0-6-0STs, Nos 68006 and 68012 at Middleton Top - 30 April 1967.

and beam engine are still there. From this point the line, as originally built, ran some 25 miles across the top of the Peaks in a north-westerly direction to Whaley Bridge, just north of Buxton. Mineral traffic was the sole reason for its existence.

The photographs chosen show a selection from that day and are in sequence for a trip from Middleton Top to Parsley Hay, although they are of different trains. The special I travelled on was the first of the day and organised by W A Camwell, a railway photographer who is owed a debt by every enthusiast for the Stephenson Locomotive Society. Two beautifully turned-out J94, 0-6-0STs Nos 68006 and 68012 were the motive power and the 100 Society members on board were accommodated in six assorted brake vans. Having arrived empty at Middleton Top, the two locomotives needed

'The opportunity to actually ride over the 1 in 14 incline in a steam-hauled train fell into the 'very rare' category.'
BR J94 0-6-0ST, No 68006 double heading No 68012 on brake van special climbing 1 in 14 Hopton Incline - 30 April 1967.

'... stone walls which were constructed to form 'embankments' ...'
BR J94 0-6-0STs, Nos 68006 and 68012 between Hopton and Parsley Hay on SLS special - 30 April 1967.

to take water and run round the train. The supply of water for locomotives was a problem on the Cromford and High Peak and improvisation was very much the order of the day on this line. Here we see the two saddle tanks filling up from an unusual 'water tower' which appears to have been constructed from a life-expired Lancashire boiler.

Leaving Middleton Top, the line soon passed through a short tunnel and the 1 in 14 incline at Hopton came into view. The incline was the 'draw' for the special trips. The opportunity actually to ride over the 1 in 14 incline in a steam-hauled train fell into the 'very rare' category. Today it is still possible to traverse Hopton Incline as part of the High Peak trail. The difference is in the means of travel; the rails are gone and it's now mountain bikes or Shanks' pony. The photograph of the steam-shrouded train charging the bank gives some idea of the effort needed to climb. Even though in this particular view the load was only four brake vans, the train stalled on the bank and had to be split into two in order to reach the top. This produced a ratio of 1:1 with two locomotives hauling two brake vans.

As the journey to Parsley Hay continued, another peculiarity of the line was traversed. This was the stone walls which were constructed to form 'embankments' of a substantial height. At the top they were only wide enough for the single track and the vertical walls were buttressed to avoid collapse. This buttressing gives the impression of not being part of the original construction, but became necessary at a later date. The two sequential scenes of the special traversing these stone-built embankments show the two saddle tanks coasting round the sharp curve at the start of such an embankment and then opening up to keep the train moving.

By now it had become a glorious day which demonstrated another of the problems in keeping the line operational. I was sitting in the sun on the flat open end of a brake van as the train crept around another impossible curve with all wheels squealing. Suddenly I became aware of myriads of steel filings cascading from the wheels and reflecting in the sun. It was not a momentary sight, but continued the whole 20 or 25 seconds that the train took to travel round the curve.

'... the vertical walls were buttressed to avoid collapse.' BR J94 0-6-0STs, Nos 68006 and 68012 running across stone-built embankment between Hopton and Parsley Hay on SLS brake van special - 30 April 1967.

'... water for the locomotives was a problem to the end.' BR J94 0-6-0STs, Nos 68006 and 68012 taking water from water tenders during an SLS brake van special run over the Cromford and High Peak - 30 April 1967.

The concluding scenes again show that water for the locomotives was a problem to the end. The limestone hills simply absorbed the rainfall like blotting paper, which then drained deep into underground rivers. There were no streams, rivers, ponds or springs for a handy natural supply. The problem was solved along the route by water trains made up from old locomotive tenders modified to carry the maximum amount of water. Filling of the saddle tanks by gravity through a 2 inch hose was a slow business and took an inordinate period of time. It took so long that I felt the engines were using it faster than it was going into the saddle tanks. Eventually, after a certain amount of anxious discussion among the railway staff, we all entrained and carried on to the limit of the special train's run at the junction at Parsley Hay, before returning again to Cromford.

'... anxious discussion among
the railway staff...'
BR J94 0-6-0STs, Nos 68006 and
68012 taking water from water
tenders during an SLS brake van
special run over the Cromford
and High Peak - 30 April 1967.

RAILS TO CARLISLE

One of the best-known railway junctions to railway enthusiasts is Carlisle. Even today, after all the rationalisation that has taken place over the last 30 years, it is still possible to arrive in Carlisle over a surprising number of different routes. On our trip north into and out of Carlisle we will stay with the original through route of the West Coast main line. The first scene is just south of Penrith on a section of line where, in days of steam haulage, express passenger trains would regularly top the 90mph mark. Steam running downhill at that speed comes across great on cine but makes little impact on a still. No smoke, no steam and you have to be lucky to get it in focus and sharp. Uphill it is different, which is what we have here. An ex-LMS 4F 0-6-0, BR No 44081, one of a few fitted with a tender cab. It is steadily working its way south up the 1 in 125 gradient towards Shap with 20 empty 16T mineral wagons and a brake van. I suspect that it was heading to

'... steadily working its way south up the 1 in 125 gradient towards Shap ...'
Ex-LMS, 4F 0-6-0 BR No 44081 just south of Penrith - 20 September 1963

'... hauling an up-freight with a type of container as good as forgotten today.'
Ex-LMS Class 5 4-6-0, BR No 45297 on an up-freight just north of Penrith - 9 September 1963.

'With the road still downhill *Atlas* was in full flight for Carlisle.'
Ex-LMS Jubilee Class 4-6-0, BR No 45737 *Atlas* on a down express to the North just north of Penrith - 9 September 1963.

load at a quarry served by a line known as mineral siding. The date was 20 September, 1963 and the weather was fine but that was no guarantee that the next day would not have rain driving straight into the face of the driver making the tender cab doubly welcome.

From just south of Penrith to just north of Penrith, time to park the car for an afternoon break. Find somewhere close to the railway and it could be a pleasant change from a long drive. Apart from a level stretch for a couple of miles near Plumpton, the line falls steadily towards Carlisle. The 9 September 1963 was another fine day and, while I took a short break, it was broken to watch and record trains passing. The second of our pictures shows another ex-LMS locomotive, Class 5 4-6-0 BR No 45297. This is hauling an up freight with a type of container as good as forgotten today – a complete train of white painted insulated containers on flat trucks. All the containers were as clean and smart as those next to the locomotive, the complete anthithesis of the popular concept of a 1960s freight train. The following scene at this pleasant rural stop-over shows a down express. In keeping with the first two it is another ex-LMS locomotive, a Jubilee Class 4-6-0 BR No 45737 *Atlas*. The passage of the down-express trains to Carlisle was hardly checked by Penrith which only had a maximum speed restriction of 60mph. With the road still downhill *Atlas* was in full flight for Carlisle. Time to pack up the picnic hamper and follow *Atlas* to Carlisle.

When I visited Carlisle with colour film in the Agfa the traffic and locomotives had changed out of all recognition from the days when I stood on Citadel station as a teenager in 1947. By the early 1960s you no longer saw Gresley Pacifics in the bay platforms at the south end of the station on the Carlisle to Newcastle trains. Nor at the bays in the north end of the station were there any of the old North British or LNER 4-4-0s on the stopping trains. One thing did not appear to have changed and that was the endless to-ing and fro-ing of tank engines shunting. The first of these shown here is an Ivatt LMS-designed 2MT 2-6-2T BR No 41264 on 26 April 1966. This is a sister engine to the one from which the footplate scene was taken on the Southern Region Lymington branch. From this shot, it is possible better to appreciate the size of the cab and the driver's point of view in allowing my presence on the footplate on the strict understanding I kept out of his side of the cab.

The usual engine seen shunting at Carlisle was the ubiquitous Class 3F 0-6-0T, now commonly referred to as a 'Jinty' tank. The example seen in the foreground is BR No 47326 but no record was kept of its sister in the background. By the date of this photograph, 9 September 1963, they were seldom seen in as attractive condition as this example. Today's multiple unit trains have overtaken the need for trains to be marshalled by station pilots, and greatly reduced the movement and interest as a result.

'One thing did not appear to have changed and that was the endless to-ing and fro-ing of tank engines shunting.'
An Ivatt LMS-designed 2MT 2-6-2T, BR No 41264 on station duties at Carlisle - 26 April 1966.

'The usual engine seen shunting at Carlisle was the ubiquitous Class 3F 0-6-0T, now commonly referred to as a 'Jinty' tank.' An ex-LMS 3F Class 0-6-0T, BR No 47326 at Carlisle - 9 September 1963.

'With a total of only ten locomotives in the class they were not an engine you would expect to see very often, yet ...' British Rail Clan Class Standard Light Pacific No 72009 *Clan Stewart* running light towards Carlisle Citadel station - 16 April 1964.

Continuing the journey north, the car is left behind and the train taken. Before leaving on the down *Waverley* for Edinburgh, the wheel tapper worked his way along the train. This type of train inspection during the journey was common and made for leisurely station stops. Leaving Carlisle and heading north on 16 April 1964, the train met and passed BR 6P5F Clan Class 4-6-2 Light Pacific No 72009 *Clan Stewart*. With a total of only ten locomotives in the class, they were not an engine you would expect to see very often, yet they turned up on a regular basis on the old LMS lines anywhere between Aberdeen and Birmingham. Photographs from the windows of moving trains at another coming towards you do not make for the best results. Apart from the nearness of the two trains in passing, today there are few trains from which you could even attempt to do so and unfortunately, you certainly would not expect to click the shutter on a similar subject.

BEATTOCK

Beattock - a name to conjure with and the obstacle for locomotives north of the border. On the former Caledonian Railway and subsequently the LMS, it sat at the bottom of the incline of the same name. The incline, of not less than 10 miles of gradient never easier than 1 in 88 and as steep as 1 in 69 in parts, is set in the beautiful countryside of the Lowther Hills. It was too remote to attract the numbers of enthusiasts found at the better known Lickey Incline between Bristol and Birmingham and consequently was never given the coverage that its uniqueness warranted.

I took all the photographs used on 20 September 1963 and the first scene was taken looking south from an overbridge some 400 or 500 yards north of the station. The rising plume of steam and smoke show just how busy it was that day. Banking engines were the mainstay of the locomotives allocated to the shed. At the date of this scene, they were ex-LMS Fairburn 2-6-4Ts. This shed was a low-roofed, two-road building which can be seen directly behind the signal box in the middle of the photograph. The lofty

'... rising plumes of steam and smoke show just how busy it was that day.'
Beattock station and locomotive depot from the north - 20 September 1963.

'... a little seen BR Standard locomotive from a class of only 20.'
BR 3MT Class 2-6-0 No 77009, at Beattock - 20 September 1963.

'A white-faced driver was leaning as far out of the cab window as he could ...'
Ex-LMS Class 5 4-6-0, BR No 45061 on an up freight, speeding through Beattock - 20 September 1963.

signal in front of the box was necessary, in order that drivers coming down the bank could see the signal over the bridge from which the photograph was taken.

The second picture was taken from the station itself and has been included because it illustrates a little seen BR Standard locomotive from a class of only 20. Seen here is Class 3MT, 2-6-0, No 77009 running light through Beattock station. Behind the locomotive is the corrugated iron structure forming the coal bench for coaling engines. This was typical of the labour intensive practices which the railways had inherited from the day of their inception, and contributed greatly to the demise of steam.

Turning round, and looking north towards the incline itself, we see a freight running past the old Caledonian Railway signal box. The engine is ex-LMS Class 5 4-6-0 BR No 45061, on up freight to Carlisle. A white-faced driver was leaning as far out of the cab window as he could, looking for the next signal. The train ran through the station at a speed I cannot remember having seen matched by any other loose-coupled freight. After that moment of excitement, we turn to an interesting engine standing dead at the north end of the locomotive yard. This was the only Caledonian locomotive I saw that day, it being one of the CR 812 Class 0-6-0s, BR No 57568. The slim boiler, sparse cab and long low tender, all contrive to give this otherwise mundane 0-6-0 freight engine a distinct style and rakish air.

To conclude, a shot of one of the Fairburn ex-LMS 2-6-4T engines banking a freight train up the incline, which I was unable to identify. The air at Beattock seemed filled continuously with the 'crows' between train engine and banker when they started from the loop running right round the outside of the complex. There was a tangible air of excitement imparted as the crews of the two engines 'talked' to one another. The sequence of calls laid down is quite brief and to the point, but memory says that they were repeated more than once. Eventually the train would be on the move, both engines hard at work, with 10 miles to go before any chance to slacken the graft.

'... slim boiler, sparse cab and long low tender ...'
Ex-CR 812 Class 0-6-0 BR No 57568 at Beattock - 20 September 1963.

'The air at Beattock seemed filled continuously with the 'crows' between train engine and banker ...'
Ex-LMS Fairburn 2-6-4T, banking freight up Beattock - 20 September 1963.

HAWICK

Hawick (pronounced Hoick!) at the time of the photographs in this section, was a small town on the Waverley route of the old North British Railway. The Waverley route ran from Edinburgh to Carlisle, a distance of 96 miles by rail, with Hawick some 53 miles from Edinburgh. Although steeply graded and sharply curved, it used to be a main line railway in the full sense of the phrase.

From the Midland and North British Railways of the late 1870s, through LMS and LNER days and into British Rail until the middle 1960s the Waverley route had through express trains between the English and Scottish capitals. I used the line regularly between London and Edinburgh because the through sleeper had a timing that was more conducive to sleep than those from Kings Cross. With regard to the latter, there was a period in the 1960s when the East Coast line from London to Edinburgh had sleeping car trains doing the run in six hours. Such a timing, when the passenger could find himself booked into a pre-war vintage sleeping carriage, did not prepare you for the day ahead. This is not a criticism of the superb Gresley-designed coaching stock, but the designer had probably not envisaged 100mph running with his sleeping carriages.

Eventually the consequences of the Beeching report reached out to the Waverley route. Once Beeching had directed that closure was to occur, efforts to kill the line were quite unbelievable. There came the day when I found that although the sleeper ran through from St Pancras to Edinburgh (Waverley), you were not allowed to book a through berth. My way of travel was not complying with the new order. Positive action by British Railways in order that the loadings decreased ultimately 'justified' reductions in the timetable and eventual closure of the line.

While the line was open it always provided great interest to me and no doubt any other visiting enthusiast. I had first visited and photographed steam at Hawick in the black and white days of August 1947. As seen in this section, even in the running down period, Hawick would provide the unexpected. The first two scenes were both taken outside the locomotive depot on 31 August 1964. In the first, I achieved the unusual by framing two locomotives with consecutive numbers while in service. These locomotives were BR 2MT Class 2-6-0s, Nos 78047 and 78048. Within the BR Standard

locomotive design, there were three separate classes of 2-6-0s. All three classes are found within this book and those examples seen here are from the smallest design of engine. With their sister design in the form of the 2MT 2-6-2T they were also the least powerful with a rated tractive effort of 18,515 lb. They were neat and tidy looking engines and as long as they were kept in a presentable condition, the lined black livery suited them well. There were a number of lightly loaded branches of the Waverley route which no doubt they were well suited to operate. The most interesting of these, to me at least, had, however, closed before they had been built. That line ran from Ricarton Junction, some 11 or 12 miles south of Hawick, to

'... I achieved the unusual by framing two locomotives with consecutive numbers while in service.'
BR 2MT Class 2-6-0s Nos 78047 and 78048 at Hawick locomotive shed - 31 August 1964.

Hexham across the border. The section of that branch had been closed between Ricarton Junction and Bellingham as early as 1951, two years before the 78XXX class were built.

Also recorded that day on Hawick shed was an example of the BR Standard 2-6-4T No 80113. Again this shows that when the BR lined black livery was kept clean, a locomotive could look very smart. Books on the old London & North Western Railway often refer to the 'blackberry' black finish that was given to their locomotives. Those who recorded in print their impressions of the old L&NWR locomotives in the pre-grouping era may well have seen a finish similar to that shown here. What colour is black? Here, well polished, no doubt with a mixture of oil and paraffin, and with the blue sky reflecting off the engine adding its own ingredient - is this what all those L&NWR engines looked like?

The last of our scenes at Hawick was taken on 16 April 1964, a few months earlier than those already shown. Here was a typical case of Hawick providing the unexpected. The locomotive is one of Gresley's V2 Class 2-6-2, BR No 60813 - unusual in that it was, I believe, the only member of the V2 Class which had that curious form of smoke deflector around the chimney. This photograph was taken from a carriage window of the down 'Waverley' from St Pancras as it slowed down for Hawick. The V2 was waiting to take what appears to be a fitted freight to Carlisle. Facing the crew of this engine was an unbroken climb to the summit at Whitrope. Starting at Hawick yard limits, it was 11 miles of solid slog. Apart from a few yards at 1 in 250, it was never easier than in 1 in 121 and had nearly 3 miles of 1 in 75 , all on a constantly curving line. I hope that 60813 was steaming well that day.

'... when the BR lined black
livery was kept clean, a
locomotive could look very
smart.'
**BR Standard 2-6-4T No 80113 at
Hawick locomotive shed - 31
August 1964.**

'... the only member of the V2
Class which had that curious
form of smoke deflector around
the chimney.'
**Ex-LNER V2 Class 2-6-2, BR No
60813 at Hawick - 16 April 1964.**

The Lowlands of Scotland

EDINBURGH, CARSTAIRS AND BLACK 5S

Today, the West Coast route to Edinburgh, originally put together by the old Caledonian and London & North Western Railways, has seen some major changes in the lowlands of Scotland. First, the old terminus of the Caledonian in Edinburgh at Princes Street was closed by British Rail in the early 1960s. More recently, there has been a major change at Carstairs which obviates the need for a train from Edinburgh to join the Glasgow to Carlisle main line heading in the wrong direction and requiring reversal.

The first picture was taken on 27 July 1966 from the arriving sleeper that had left St Pancras at 21.15 the evening before. This had used the Waverley route through Hawick which we have visited in the previous

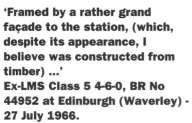

'Framed by a rather grand façade to the station, (which, despite its appearance, I believe was constructed from timber) ...'
Ex-LMS Class 5 4-6-0, BR No 44952 at Edinburgh (Waverley) - 27 July 1966.

section. My notes show that my train arrived at Edinburgh (Waverley) hauled by D34, later to be 45119, of the old Type 4 Peak Class diesels at 07.25. Allowing a minute between taking the photograph and stopping in the station enables the time of the photograph to be established as 07.24. Framed by a rather grand façade to the station (which, despite its appearance, I believe was constructed from timber) is seen an ex-LMS Class 5 4-6-0, BR No 44952. Edinburgh (Waverley) is one enormous island platform station, with the two outside platform faces allowing trains to run through the station, while between these two platforms room is available at each end of the station for a whole series of lengthy bay platforms. On that morning, No 44952 was shunting the bay platforms at the east end of the station which at the time were used extensively for the handling of Post Office mail and parcel traffic.

From the east end of the station to the west end and back in time a few months to 25 April 1966. By that date, Edinburgh, Princes Street, station had been closed and all traffic had been diverted into Edinburgh, Waverley. The train was the 17.20 to Carstairs and was a through train to Liverpool. Seen here, ex-LMS Class 5 4-6-0, BR No 45295 is at the head of

'I suppose that the weather could be fickle enough to warrant a snow plough between Edinburgh and Carstairs at that time of year ...'
Ex-LMS Class 5 4-6-0, BR No 45295 at Edinburgh (Waverley) waiting to leave with the 17.20 to Liverpool via Carstairs - 25 April 1966.

only three coaches. On reaching Carstairs, the Edinburgh portion would be attached to a Glasgow to Liverpool train and the two sections would continue as one. Late afternoon in April, under the canopy of a station built at the bottom of a drained loch, is not the best place for photography. That, coupled with an almost total lack of colour makes this scene very drab in contrast to that taken from the other end of the station. What makes this scene of interest are the peculiarities shown. As with No 44952 in the first photograph, the lamp iron originally located at the 12 o'clock position on the smokebox has been moved to the 3 o'clock position. This was changed on safety grounds due to the spread of overhead electrification which was already installed on the Glasgow suburban routes out of Glasgow Central. The other interesting peculiarity is, of course, the snow plough. To see a steam locomotive fitted with a snow plough always gave me an extra feeling of awareness of the demands of running a railway. To see an engine fitted with a snow plough sweep through a station was an event which would be guaranteed to be remembered. I suppose that the weather could be fickle enough to warrant a snow plough between Edinburgh and Carstairs at that time of year, but it certainly was not the case on 25 April 1966 which was a pleasant evening, as will be seen when we arrive at Carstairs.

At Carstairs the train ran through the station in the direction of Glasgow. There it would wait until the arrival of the Glasgow portion which would run into the station. Then the Edinburgh would be slowly backed onto the end of the Glasgow section and coupled up into one train. The third photograph was taken from the vestibule window of what had been the last coach of an ex-Edinburgh train as it was being backed into Carstairs station. Carstairs was another island station formed by a broad single platform with all the station buildings contained between two platform faces. The last coach of the Glasgow portion can be seen directly ahead, and to the right another ex-LMS Class 5 4-6-0, BR No 45217 on a northbound parcels. From Carstairs, the train ran down Beattock and past the station and locomotive depot which we visited a few pages back. However, on 25 April 1966, that was a diesel-hauled train to the south and we will turn to the steam attractions to the north of Edinburgh.

'... was taken from the vestibule window of what had been the last coach of an ex-Edinburgh train as it was being backed into Carstairs station.' Carstairs station taken from the north and looking south, photographed from the window of an Edinburgh to Liverpool train as it was being connected to the Glasgow to Liverpool portion. Heading a northbound parcels is ex-LMS Class 5 4-6-0, BR No 45217 - 25 April 1966.

PICK-UP FREIGHT AT KIRKLISTON

Kirkliston may be found just to the east of Edinburgh and the line shown here was originally part of the old North British Railway's Ratho to South Queensferry branch. Driving past on 10 September 1963, the sight of smoke and steam from the cutting below was reason enough to stop and investigate. Appropriately, I found an ex-North British 0-6-0, British Railways Class J36, No 65327 going about its daily business with a pick-up freight. In the heyday of steam, every wayside station played host to the pick-up goods. Anything and everything that a community required from the outside world would arrive on the pick-up goods, which would then depart

'... ex-North British 0-6-0, British Railways Class J36, No 65327 going about its daily business with a pick-up freight.'
J36, No 65327 at Kirkliston - 10 September 1963.

with the corresponding outgoing freight from that community. Obviously the goods were varied and on a busy section a train could run to 20 or 30 wagons at a time. Contrary to popular impression, it was not a slow and easy going business. From experience, I had learnt that you took your railway photograph at the first opportunity, so the first photograph was taken from the top of the cutting, just as soon as I could get No 65327 in the viewfinder.

Although it was a sunny day, you can see that the cab roof is fitted with a tarpaulin with the tender modified by a tubular framework for the tarpaulin's attachment. Pick-up freights could be expected to do a good deal of tender first running, both from shunting at each stop and on the return trip when they would, as often as not, be unable to turn the locomotive.

The J36 shunted off and I hung around for a while to see if there was to be an opportunity for a further photograph. In time she returned, coupled to a container loaded on a flat truck, as opposed to the fruit van in the first scene. Dutifully posed, No 65327 demonstrates just how much character the common, humble freight-hauling 0-6-0 could show. Sadly today, the pick-up freight is no more, nor is the carriage of fresh fruit by train, and No 65327 was withdrawn from service by British Rail in November 1965.

'The J36 shunted off and I hung around for a while ... In time she returned, coupled to a container loaded on a flat truck ...'
Ex-North British 0-6-0, British Railways Class J36, No 65327 at Kirkliston - 10 September 1963.

Farther North and Farther North

In the Kingdom of Fife

A momentary stop, at Cupar, on our journey farther north. It was here, having taken a photograph of a J38 Class 0-6-0 shunting the goods yard, the driver had rebuked me with the words "it's not Fifeshire but the Kingdom of Fife". By such gems is the railway enthusiasts' knowledge of Scottish history and geography extended.

Just a single scene, taken on 24 March 1964, while I was leaning over the fence at the back of the down-platform of Cupar station. The object of my interest was BR-built B1 Class 4-6-0 No 61346. Built in April 1949 of a class of 410 locomotives, 61346 was one of only ten which were built at the Gorton Works of the old Great Central Railway. The engine is well turned-out and not just from a cleanliness aspect. Apart from the safety valves lightly blowing off, there is not a trace of steam to be seen elsewhere. It must have been disheartening for those responsible for maintaining this engine to find that it was withdrawn within three months of this photograph being taken.

To me this shot brings back thoughts of all those engines seen, from the station platform, while they shunted the pick-up goods. It also shows the lines of a much underrated locomotive; 410 in a class which has never been given the credit it warranted. Reliable, free steaming and as capable or more as any other 4-6-0 when it came to hauling a 10 or 11 coach train. Perhaps it was because it was an LNER design, from the post group company which on a day-to-day basis, was the least glamorous of the big four. Here is the perfect steam era scene from the LNER era. The 'typical' station, goods yard, the North British signal box, the Edwardian-style lamp-post (which so nearly ruins everything by sprouting out of the funnel), the loading bay, the telegraph wires to the signal box, the point with the interlaced sleepers and of course, the B1 4-6-0.

'... this shot brings back thoughts of all those other engines seen from the station platform, while they shunted the pick-up goods.'
BR-built B1 Class 4-6-0 No 61346 at Cupar - 24 March 1964.

FORT WILLIAM RELICS

When I was a teenage railway enthusiast in the 1940s, the train of the LNER was not the *Flying Scotsman* but the sleeper that left Kings Cross at 8.00pm. Bound for Aberdeen with a portion for Fort William, it was the train you waited to see before cycling home in the twilight. Always loaded to at least 15 carriages, sometimes 16, 17 or even 18, it was a sight to see as it climbed north out of London. Anything else that followed was sheer anti-climax.

To a youngster whose knowledge of Scotland had been a single day in Hawick, the 8.00pm *Aberdonian* was the stuff from which dreams were made. However, it was not Aberdeen but the Fort William portion that captured the imagination. By the time I had freedom and ability to travel wherever I wished, Fort William and the line from Queen Street had been dieselised. Imagine my surprise when, on 13 September 1963, I found a steam locomotive on Fort William shed. Furthermore, as far as Fort William was concerned, it was a curiosity. Seen in the first photograph is ex-LMS 4F 0-6-0, BR No 44255. As it was one of the most common locomotives to be seen on the ex-LMS lines of British Rail, I could not ignore the 4F 0-6-0s' existence. Instead, I have shown an example in an unexpected situation.

The second photograph, taken on the same day at Fort William, shows a snow plough grafted onto a locomotive tender. This example has a definite air of being local manufacture and not something that was of concern to anyone south of the border. The only identification was SPT2 on the leading edge of the tender. Snow plough tender No 2 I presume. I wonder what SPT1 looked like?

'... as far as Fort William was
concerned, it was a curiosity.'
Ex-LMS 4F 0-6-0, BR No 44255 at
Fort William locomotive shed -
13 September 1963.

'... shows a snow plough grafted
onto a locomotive tender.' Snow
plough No SPT2 at Fort William -
13 September 1963.

FOREIGNERS ON THE CALEY

With the closure of Kings Cross top shed in June 1963, there was very little work left on the East Coast main line for the eleven A4 Class Pacifics still in service. During the following winter, nine of these were transferred to Scotland, although it was not until the following summer that they were all found back in service. Over the next two and a bit years they became masters of the three-hour services on the Caledonian Railway's main line between Glasgow (Buchanan Street) and Aberdeen. During the summer of 1964, I found time to visit Buchanan Street on a day of torrential and continuous rain. I liked Buchanan Street, for a main line terminus; memory says eight platforms of which the longest might hold a 9-coach train. It had a friendly, homely atmosphere. All things are relative and you could hardly apply the same adjectives to St Enoch or Central stations.

However, on 5 September 1964, I made my way to Buchanan Street and was rewarded by seeing two Gresley A4 Pacifics. The first had brought in the 1.30pm from Aberdeen and the second took out the 5.30pm return service. The state of these two engines made me feel quite sick, even though at this time filthy locomotives were an occupational hazard for locomotive men. I was devastated; not only did I not bother to photograph the

'... could well be the last A4 I would see in service.'
Ex-LNER A4 4-6-2, BR No 60026 *Kestrel* with the 5.30pm to Aberdeen, at Buchanan Street, Glasgow - 5 September 1964.

'... better to think that *Lord Farringdon* is about to leave the shed for for the next scheduled express.'
BR A4 Class 4-6-2, No 60034 *Lord Farringdon* disabled on Perth shed - 25 August 1966.

locomotive of the 1.30 ex-Aberdeen as it backed out of the station, I did not even keep a record of its number. That left 60026 *Kestrel* at the head of 7 coaches waiting to leave on the 5.30pm to Aberdeen. Standing in the pouring rain, I reflected that in that condition their days just had to be numbered. This sad sight could well be the last A4 I would see in service. The thought prompted me to take a couple of photographs, one of which has been used to illustrate this section for comparison with what was to follow.

During the next eighteen months, word came back that the A4 Pacifics were not in terminal decline but were enjoying a real Indian Summer. That this was to be for a limited period, as dieselisation continued to spread, was obvious. It was, therefore, less than two years later that all the gear was packed into the trusty MGA; it was time to head north once more. Aberdeen, as opposed to Glasgow, was the destination this time – after all, the East coast is supposed to be drier. The route taken was via Perth and it was on 25 August 1966 that I found A4 No 60034 *Lord Farringdon* disabled at Perth shed but in near-immaculate condition. What a difference to *Kestrel* less than two years earlier. The shame was that as *Lord Farringdon* stood disabled and minus her tender, I believe I am correct in saying, she had run her last revenue earning run and was condemned where she stood. Put that thought away – how much better to think that *Lord Farringdon* is about to leave the shed for the next scheduled express.

Just two days later, I and the faithful Agfa, were on Aberdeen station. Not another enthusiast in sight unless it was the third person who left on the footplate of A4, No 60024 *Kingfisher*, with the 13.30 to Glasgow. I have included three separate photographs of *Kingfisher* that day at Aberdeen, as I understand that the 13.30 to Glasgow was the last BR passenger train in the timetable scheduled to be hauled by an A4 locomotive. At this time there was only one other A4, 60019 *Bittern*, in service and both were withdrawn before another week was out. Presumably for sentimental reasons, both locomotives were reinstated for one return trip each between Aberdeen and Glasgow. *Bittern* did the trip on 3 September 1966 and *Kingfisher* on 13 September 1966. I was not there to witness those runs but I imagine that many a railway enthusiast was in my place. Where they were when the curtain should have come down on the A4 saga, goodness only knows.

From my vantage point on Aberdeen station, first I am able to show you 60024 backing down onto the train. Again, the locomotive is beautifully turned out, with a deep polish to the paintwork. One of the problems in preserving a true colour image for posterity is clearly evident; like the sea, locomotives in green will always reflect the blue of the sky on a clear sunny day.

'... the locomotive is beautifully turned out, with a deep polish to the paintwork.'
BR A4 Class 4-6-2 No 60024 *Kingfisher* at Aberdeen, backing down onto the 13.30 to Glasgow - 27 August 1966.

While the engine was coupled to the train, it was round to the departure platform for a shot of the left-hand side of *Kingfisher*. By now, the locomotive was not only coupled up to the train, but had also acquired a second, spotless, white lamp - this time, above the right-hand buffer to complete the express head code. Back round to the original vantage point in time for a third picture of *Kingfisher* leaving Aberdeen with the last passenger train in the timetable to be hauled by an A4 Pacific. A little sad, I retired for a late lunch taken at a table on the first floor of a café overlooking the northerly approach to the station. There, while tucking into an omelette, what should appear from the station and then disappear back again, but another A4! A certain urgency came over the finishing of the meal, by which time there was no sign of steam in the station. I jumped into the car and drove round to Ferryhill locomotive depot.

'... it was round to the departure platform for a shot of the left-hand side of *Kingfisher*.' BR A4 Class 4-6-2, No 60024 *Kingfisher* at Aberdeen at the head of the 13.30 to Glasgow - 27 August 1966.

'... the last passenger train in the timetable to be hauled by an A4 Pacific.'
BR Class A4 4-6-2 No. 60024 *Kingfisher* leaving Aberdeen at the head of the 13.30 to Glasgow - 27 August 1966.

Ferryhill with ten locomotive roads, was a large depot by any standards. The shed, when built, was shared by the Caledonian Railway with seven roads and the North British Railway, who had the use of the remaining three roads. This was continued, after grouping, by their successors, the LMS and LNER respectively. From LMS days the shed had suffered a serious decline, not having anything like the allocation the size of shed warranted – only 14 LMS engines in total in 1945. That number of locomotives would have been riches indeed on 27 August 1966, but the sight of A4 No 60019 *Bittern* standing outside the shed was reward enough. The only problem was from a photographic point of view; half the locomotive was in sun and the other half in shade. Further, there was no expectation of her moving with the front of the stream line casing open while the smokebox was cleared of char. It was very much a case of making the best of a poor situation.

Investigation of the shed yielded an unexpected reward, another 4-6-2 locomotive. This was BR No 60532 *Blue Peter*, a Peppercorn A2 Class locomotive, ordered by the LNER and completed after nationalisation in 1948. Gently simmering steam, *Blue Peter* was very much a live engine, but again in an almost hopeless position for photographing. A last look and back to the MGA – steam photography was over for the day. *Kestrel*, *Lord Farringdon* and *Kingfisher* had appointments with the scrap merchants' torch; *Bittern* and *Blue Peter* survived for preservation.

'... while the smokebox was cleared of char.'
BR A4 Class 4-6-2, No 60019 *Bittern* on Ferryhill shed, Aberdeen - 27 August 1966.

'Investigation of the shed yielded an unexpected reward ...'
BR A2 Class 4-6-2, No 60532, *Blue Peter* on Ferryhill shed, Aberdeen - 27 August 1966.

Back Down the East Coast

THE NORTH EAST INDUSTRIAL HEARTLAND

Newcastle was a railway centre where I always seemed to find myself with time to watch the trains at the wrong time of day for photography. Central station and the goods avoiding lines with the cramped junctions just off each end of the station, resulted in a constant and fascinating parade of passenger trains and heavy freight. Today, the famous and much photographed track layout has been simplified out of all recognition, and the parade reduced almost solely to the passenger traffic. Heavy freight used to be the backbone of the traffic in days of steam, not just for Newcastle but for the entire North East. The old pre-group company, the North Eastern Railway, built considerable numbers of large, powerful, slow, slogging freight engines for work in the North East. These locomotives were so successful in hauling heavy freight, that examples lasted almost to the end of steam itself.

'... slowly grinding to a halt as it waited for the right of way.'
Ex-North Eastern Railway Q6 Class 0-8-0, BR No 63453 on the goods avoiding line at Newcastle Central - 27 May 1965.

The first two photographs show a typical freight on the goods avoiding lines past Central station. The locomotive is an ex-North Eastern Railway Q6 Class 0-8-0, BR No 63453. Built in 1920, it survived almost to the end of steam on BR, eventually being withdrawn in October 1966. In the first scene, No 63453 is slowly grinding to a halt as it waited for the right of way. Behind the engine, the water tank and column are reminders of the extent of the installations that the steam locomotives required in order to operate. Provision such as this had to be made at all strategic points on the system and not only at engine sheds.

The second view is taken from the rear, as No 63453 slowly pulls away across the junction to take the Elswick and Scotswood line, giving the fireman some relief as the line was on a falling gradient for the next few miles. This also shows the junction at the west end of Newcastle Central. The restrictions imposed on the track layout of a major junction in a city centre are all too evident. This added to the operating problems, which were compounded by the sheer length of time that trains such as this freight took to navigate the crossing.

'... slowly pulls away across the junction to take the Elswick and Scotswood line ...'
Ex-North Eastern Railway Q6 0-8-0, BR No 63453 on the goods avoiding line at Newcastle Central - 27 May 1965.

'... has been carefully brought to a halt under a water filling point.'
Ex-North Eastern Railway J27 Class 0-6-0, BR No 65873 at West Hartlepool station - 31 August 1966.

We then move from Newcastle south down the coast to West Hartlepool, which was also very much part of the North Eastern Railway in pre-grouping days. Shown is an ex-North Eastern J27 Class 0-6-0, BR No 65873 in West Hartlepool station on 31 August 1966. It was to be another six or seven years before the vast suburb spawned by Hartlepool officially became known by the name of its parent. By that time, the original Hartlepool station, the other side of the docks, no longer had a passenger service. Close observation of this scene will show that No 65873 has been carefully brought to a halt under a water filling point. The supply had been brought out along the girders and the hose can be seen lifted out of the way of passing trains. Like all ordinary water columns, the operating valve was on the platform.

West Hartlepool needed a substantial locomotive shed to provide services for the surrounding area. The shed was developed on the most constricted of sites, where the line to Middlesbrough came out almost to the foreshore. The shed had grown in two separate sections, one a straight road shed and the other a round house, separated, if my memory is correct, by a level crossing. Here, on 31 August 1966, I photographed another member of the Q6 Class 0-8-0, this time BR No 63412. Built in 1919, this locomotive had been withdrawn from service only the month before I stopped by and recorded its last days.

'The shed was developed on the most constricted of sites, where the line to Middlesbrough came out almost to the foreshore.' Ex-North Eastern Railway Q6 0-8-0, BR No 63412 at West Hartlepool shed - 31 August 1966.

YORKSHIRE COAL

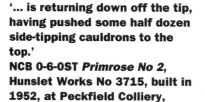

'... is returning down off the tip, having pushed some half dozen side-tipping cauldrons to the top.'
NCB 0-6-0ST *Primrose No 2*, Hunslet Works No 3715, built in 1952, at Peckfield Colliery, Micklefield - April 1972.

For a number of years after the demise of steam on British Rail, it was still possible to see steam locomotives working hard on a regular daily basis, if you knew where to look. These engines were, of course, the industrial variety of which the National Coal Board still had a good number working. One place where steam was still used daily in the early 1970s was at Peckfield Colliery, Micklefield which is a few miles due east of Leeds. My itinerary at the time, took me past Micklefield each week in the early evening.

Occasionally, if the weather was fine in the summer, and notwithstanding the fact that I still had a good 2 ½ hours' drive in front of me, I would turn off the A1 and stop for a while. The illustrations are typical

'... shows the extent of the care taken in the finish to so many industrial locomotives.'
NCB 0-6-0T No S.100 built by Hudswell Clarke, Works No 1822 in 1949, at Peckfield Colliery, Micklefield - April 1972.

of those taken during these stops, and the first shows NCB 0-6-0ST *Primrose No 2* in April 1972. This locomotive, Works No 3715, was built by Hunslet in 1952. It was subsequently preserved and is to be found working on the Yorkshire Dales Railway at Embsay.

Primrose No 2 is seen here returning down off the tip having pushed some half dozen side-tipping cauldrons to the top where the slag from the colliery would have been emptied and then spread by a bulldozer. There were two locomotives which worked the tip during my visits and the second was NCB 0-6-0T No S.100. This locomotive was built by Hudswell Clarke, Works No 1822, in 1949 and the first view shows the only time that I was able to get a shot of the left-hand side of either of these engines. What I like about this photograph is that it shows the extent of the care taken in the finish to so many industrial locomotives. The lining in particular has a depth of colour in the evening sunlight, giving it the impression of being gold leaf. In this instance it was marshalling some empty cauldrons for refilling.

The third photograph shows No S.100 at the identical spot where *Primrose No 2* had been photographed. It is also running down from the tip with empty cauldrons. Both engines always pushed the cauldrons up in front of them with the locomotive facing up the gradient. While this kept the maximum level of water over the crown of the firebox, it also meant I was only able to get rear views of the two engines. In time, the yard personnel came to recognise me and, when they discovered that I came from the sinful south, it was hinted that if I could obtain a selection of *Playboy* and *Mayfair* type magazines, I would have the freedom of the footplate.

In due course, I returned armed with the appropriate bribe - acquired, I might add, second-hand from the assistant of my local model shop - and the agreement was duly honoured. Unfortunately, this came to an untimely end as one day I arrived to be told, with considerable disappointment, that footplate rides were finished. It transpired that the previous week the NCB equivalent of a passed fireman was at the regulator on a wet and nasty day. Going up the incline to the top of the tip, they slipped to a standstill and the driver not only failed to restart, but found himself being pushed down the incline at ever increasing speed. As one, the crew abandoned the footplate.

'... it is also running down from the tip with empty cauldrons.' NCB 0-6-0T No S.100, built by Hudswell Clarke, Works No 1822, in 1949, at Peckfield Colliery, Micklefield - 19 April 1972.

'... they slipped to a standstill and the driver not only failed to restart, but found himself being pushed down the incline ...'
NCB 0-6-0ST *Primrose No 2*, Hunslet Works No 3715, built in 1952, at Peckfield Colliery, Micklefield - April 1972.

'A nice sunny evening, but it shows the nature of the work demanded from a typical industrial locomotive ...' NCB 0-6-0T No S.100, built by Hudswell Clarke, Works No 1822 in 1949 at Peckfield Colliery, Micklefield - April 1972.

My informant described how the engine appeared, crewless, from under the footbridge at an unbelievable speed and ran through a set of trailing points set against it, without derailing. Once on the level, the engine slowed down quite sharply but not sharp enough to avoid hitting a second engine about to shunt the transfer sidings with British Rail. This second locomotive was hit sufficiently hard for it to be put into the workshop. The reason for the runaway slowing now became apparent. No sooner had the runaway hit the second engine than it took off again, still driverless. The driver had abandoned the engine with the regulator wide open in full forward gear as though half-way up that ferocious incline. It did not repeat the performance, though, as the points had been changed for the transfer siding. The return trip ended with it running full tilt into a waiting coal train and "we were knee deep in the stuff and it's taken all week to clear up".

I, of course, was left thereafter to photograph the locomotives climbing the tip from the yard below. Two of the resulting photographs illustrate this section with the first showing the runaway *Primrose No 2* with the dent resulting from the escapade visible on the rear of the coal bunker. The last photograph in this section is an earlier picture of S.100 about a quarter of the way up the incline. A nice sunny evening, but it shows the nature of the work demanded from a typical industrial locomotive which resulted in the episode described earlier.

SUNDAY MORNING AT RETFORD

The opportunity to make a small diversion from the planned route while on holiday gave rise to a pleasant hour's break at Retford in Nottinghamshire. It was at this point that two main lines, from pre-grouping times, crossed one another on the level. The earliest line was the Sheffield to Grimsby line built by the forerunner of the Great Central – the Manchester, Sheffield and Lincolnshire Railway. This was subsequently crossed by the Great Northern line from Kings Cross to Doncaster. Today a diversion has been built and the old Great Central line runs underneath the Kings Cross to Doncaster route. However, at the time of my visit, on 30 August 1964, the original flat crossing was still in existence, and both were very busy lines and had been for more than 100 years.

The interest at Retford at this date arose from the fact that the old Great Central/LNER shed had acquired a large allocation of freight engines as a result of some intermediate rationalisation by British Rail. At times such as Christmas, when the entire railway operation shut down, there could be as many as 60 or 70 engines on shed, totally overwhelming the facilities. Even on this Sunday morning there were over 40 locomotives present, and the shed staff were scratching their heads (metaphorically speaking) in sorting out the tangle so that by the next day the engines could leave in a sequence which ensured the rota was kept.

A shed full only of freight locomotives with their unkempt appearance might be thought limited in appeal, but Retford and its locomotives had been passed on to British Rail by the old LNER, the railway whose traffic had suffered the most in the 1920s and 30s. As a result, there was none of the mass renewal programmes which standardised the locomotive fleets of the LMS and GWR or the electrification programme which decimated the locomotives of the Southern Railway. Instead, there was a great deal of modification on existing locomotives compatible with economy and tight financial control. The result was that Retford, on 30 August 1964, was almost still pure LNER, from a locomotive aspect.

Commencing in order of seniority, the oldest locomotive of the quartet shown at Retford that day is BR No 63773. Built in August 1912 as a Robinson Great Central 2-8-0 and subsequently classified by the LNER as a member of the 04 Class, it was rebuilt in 1946 into an 01 2-8-0. The

'... this class of locomotive was
the most economical type of
engine amongst the 2-8-0 freight
locomotives tested by BR in the
Interchange Trials in 1948.'
Ex-LNER O1 Class 2-8-0 BR No
63773, rebuilt from O4/3 class
by Thompson and seen at
Retford - 30 August 1964.

rebuilding scheme was part of Thompson's programme to upgrade the heavy mineral locomotive fleet without launching into an expensive programme of new locomotives. The rebuilding programme extended from the first locomotive in February 1944 until the 58th and last in October 1949. In their rebuilt form, this class of locomotive was the most economical type of engine amongst the 2-8-0 freight locomotives tested by British Rail in the Interchange Trials in 1948. Rebuilt as Class O1 and, as seen here, 63773 presented a modern appearance for an engine more than 50 years old. However, despite this appearance, 63773 only had days left before being withdrawn in October 1964.

The next oldest of the quartet was No 63651. This was an ex-ROD (Railway Operating Department) locomotive, built by Kitson & Co in March 1918. Surplus to requirement at the end of the First World War, this locomotive was acquired by the newly formed LNER in August 1925 and became another member of the O4 2-8-0 Class. As with its classmate No 63773, this engine fell under the eye of the LNER's new chief mechanical engineer, Thompson. The rebuilding of 63651 was not quite as drastic as

'No 63651 as seen here, has been modified with the Darlington standard boiler, Diagram 10A ...'
Ex-LNER O4/8 Class 2-8-0, BR No 63651 at Retford - 30 August 1964.

that of engines reclassified into the O1 Class. No 63651, as seen here, has been modified with the Darlington standard boiler Diagram 10A which left it classified as an O4/8 Class locomotive. As such, it lasted the longest of the trio of 2-8-0s shown, eventually being withdrawn in July 1965.

The most junior of the three 2-8-0s in our locomotive quartet was No 63702. Although this was another ROD locomotive built in July 1918 by R Stephenson & Co and taken in LNER stock subsequently as Class O4/3 in March 1924, it is pure Great Central. Seen here under the locomotive hoist, it is possible to get some idea just how impressive this class of locomotive was, particularly when you stood alongside one at rail level. Despite the full tender of coal, I wonder if 63702 ever worked another revenue-earning train because she was withdrawn during the next month, September 1964.

'Despite the full tender of coal, I wonder if 63702 ever worked another revenue earning train ...'
Ex-LNER O4/3 Class 2-8-0, BR No 63702 at Retford - 30 August 1964.

'This class of locomotive arose from Thompson rebuilding one of Gresley's three-cylinder K4 Class 2-6-0s ...'
K1 Class 2-6-0, BR No 62054 at Retford - 30 August 1964.

From the 2-8-0 wheel arrangement to the 2-6-0 arrangement and K1 Class locomotive 62054. This class of locomotive arose from Thompson rebuilding one of Gresley's three-cylinder K4 Class 2-6-0s into a two-cylinder form. Before nationalisation, only the rebuild was actually running although during the last year of the LNER's existence (1947) an order for 70 production models was placed with the North British Locomotive Company which were delivered in 1949 and 1950 after nationalisation of the railways. The K1s were a very versatile class of locomotives and capable of hauling and meeting the schedules of most of the express trains of the 1950s on the Eastern Region of British Rail if the regular rostered class of locomotive was unavailable. As freight engines, they were capable of lifting loads of 25% greater than the best 0-6-0 freight engines previously possessed by the LNER. Dieselisation pronounced the end for 62054 which had barely survived its fifteenth birthday when it was withdrawn in December 1964.

Great Central and London Extension

WOODFORD AND HINTON

The pre-group railway companies who formed the British Railways of their day established new centres of population solely to service their network, which became known as railway towns.

Some, such as Swindon and Crewe, became household names and large and resilient enough to withstand the crippling closures of works resulting from British Rail's nationalisation schemes.

Other centres were unknown, small, close-knit and unlucky. One such railway community was set up by the Great Central on its London extension just south of the village of Woodford Halse. The Great Central then enlarged the scope of the station and, no doubt aggravating the residents of Woodford Halse, called the station Woodford and Hinton – Hinton being the neighbouring village to Woodford Halse. The area was, and still is come to that, totally rural. The need to set up a sizeable railway

**'This was a straight road shed and was exactly the same size and to the same design as the shed built at Neasden ...'
Ex-Great Central Shed at Woodford - 28 March 1965.**

'... overshadowed by its replacement, can be seen the original brick built coaling bank ...'
Coaling facilities at Woodford locomotive depot - 3 August 1964.

community arose from the operating practice and needs of the steam locomotive which demanded a fairly substantial locomotive establishment in this vicinity. Freight locomotives required to be changed on a freight train's cross-country journey. Woodford, as it became known, served the Great Central not only with their own freight on the main line, but also with freight on and off its branch connecting with Banbury, where it met the Great Western, and the cross-country Stratford-upon-Avon and Midland Junction Railway. It became a very busy railway centre with extensive railway facilities. Just how extensive can be seen from a visit to the locomotive shed. This was a straight road shed and was exactly the same size and to the same design as the shed built at Neasden to service the London end of the extension. Seen here on 28 March 1965, the shed has an extensive selection of ex-LMS locomotives. These had become the general type of motive power found on the line at that date. Black 5, 4-6-0s and 8F 2-8-0s had more or less ousted ex-LNER classes of engine.

An even more impressive sign of the centre's importance was the servicing facilities provided with the depot. Still standing, but overshadowed by its replacement, can be seen the original brick-built coaling bank which,

'Downgraded from the express workings of the glory years ...' Ex-LMS rebuilt Royal Scot Class 4-6-0, BR No 46156 *The South Wales Borderer* at Woodford - 3 August 1964.

when built in the 1890s, was regarded as the latest and best for such a depot. That this was insufficient to meet the needs of the line during the next 50 years is shown by the later, reinforced concrete, coaling plant. The original stage, it is presumed, survived because the roof carried the water tank for the shed. The substantial building in the foreground was the provider of another important locomotive need – sand – which needed to be dried before being supplied to the engine. The date was Sunday, 3 August 1964 and although the line was still busy in the week, it was shut down on Sunday, an indication of the outlook and total closure.

Standing outside the shed that day, was LMS-rebuilt Royal Scot Class 4-6-0, BR No 46156 *The South Wales Borderer*. Downgraded from the express workings of the glory years, it had found its way to Woodford. There was not much colour to record and only the steam escaping from the cylinder stop cocks shows that it could be a working locomotive. In contrast, I have added to this section a photograph taken just off the south end of Woodford station. An immaculate ex-Midland Railway 4F Class 0-6-0, BR No 44188 is seen backing on to a Stephenson Locomotive Society special on 24 April 1965. The special had started from Birmingham Snow Hill for a run over the Stratford-upon-Avon and Midland Junction line between Stratford-upon-Avon and Woodford. As this locomotive was the best presented of all the 4F 0-6-0s which I have recorded, together with the fact that it is on the old Great Central pointing in the direction of the next section, it seemed appropriate to take the opportunity to include it.

'... backing on to a Stephenson Locomotive Society special ...' Ex-Midland Railway 4F Class 0-6-0, BR No 44188 at Woodford while working a SLS special - 24 April 1965.

JOINT RAILS WITH THE GREAT WESTERN

During the early 1960s, there was a period when once or twice a week it was necessary for me to use the Princes Risborough to Thame road. This road crosses the old Great Western and Great Central joint line between Northolt Junction and Ashendon, some nine or ten miles north-west of Princes Risborough. This section of line used to be an important and busy main line carrying the Great Western Birmingham, Wolverhampton, Shrewsbury and Birkenhead expresses. Even at the time of the scenes accompanying this section, British Rail considered that it was important enough to carry that concept before its time, the Blue Pullman. The route also carried considerable freight traffic and it was seldom that in driving along the road that a plume of smoke would not be seen to herald a passing train. Subject to various conditions, such as: I reached the bridge first; I had a few minutes to spare; the weather was OK and I had film in the camera, I would often stop and see if it was worth taking a shot.

'With the brake van barely visible at the end of the train, it is possible to get a good understanding of the amount of freight that this line used to carry.' Ex-GWR 38XX Class 2-8-0, No 3812, with a down-freight on the old Great Western and Great Central joint line between Princes Risborough and Ashendon Junction where the line is crossed by the Princes Risborough to Thame road - 24 April 1965. (All scenes in this section were taken at this point of the line.)

'..the first 12 locomotives of this class had domeless boilers. Twenty-eight years later, and goodness knows how many boiler changes, No 48010 is still fitted with a domeless boiler.' Ex-LMS 8F Class 2-8-0, BR No 48010 on up-mineral freight - 26 July 1963.

Notwithstanding all the above conditions, I find that I have a surfeit of views to choose from. I have started with a late picture because it portrays the road bridge over the line from which all other scenes were taken. Here, on 24 April 1965, we see a northbound empty mineral train being worked by ex-Great Western 38XX Class 2-8-0, No 3812. Churchward turned out the first of the class as long ago as 1903. Thirty-five years later, his successor at Swindon, Collett, decided that it was worth continuing the breed, and doubled the size of the existing fleet. The modifications, apart from the cabside window seen here, were only in detail. The 2-8-0 as a heavy freight locomotive was not going to be challenged on the Great Western. With the brake van barely visible at the end of the train, it is possible to get a good understanding of the amount of freight that this line used to carry.

Turning the clock back a bit further, the next scene shows an ex-LMS 8F 2-8-0, BR No 48010, on 26 July 1963. Another long line of 16T mineral wagons - this time they are loaded and 48010 is hauling an up-mineral freight, towards Princes Risborough. The LMS 8F 2-8-0 was introduced by Stanier in 1935 and the first 12 locomotives of this class had domeless boilers. Twenty-eight years later, and goodness knows how many boiler changes, 48010 is still fitted with a domeless boiler. The line at this point is easily graded, but generally rising against up trains. A clear exhaust from the chimney shows she was running well despite the shabby looking exterior condition,

The sister 8F 2-8-0 that follows in the next scene with another up-goods is BR No 48517, photographed on 4 September 1963. This elevated shot clearly shows the boiler fitted with a dome and top feed. The incidence of tender-first running for freight engines was more common than generally appreciated. In this example, the crew do not have the benefit of a tender cab. If it was a wet day, the best a crew could have expected was a tarpaulin stretched between cab roof and tender.

The use of a tarpaulin, with all its limitations in providing protection to the crew, is shown in the next scene. Here we have an ex-LMS Class 5 4-6-0, BR No 44932 on 4 February 1964. It was not rain that induced the 'fitting' of the tarpaulin that day, but a cold, frosty February morning. This view shows No 44932 hauling a pick-up goods, three empty 16T mineral wagons, two more loaded with coal, what appears to be a 12T five plank wagon with the load sheeted over and the guard's brake van - definitely surplus power for a train of that size. No 44932 survived to the end of steam on British Rail and has been preserved.

'... tender-first running for freight engines was more common than generally appreciated.' Ex-LMS 8F Class 2-8-0, BR No 48517 on up goods - 4 September 1963.

'The use of a tarpaulin, with all its limitations in providing protection to the crew ...' Ex-LMS Class 5 4-6-0, BR No 44932 on up pick-up goods - 4 February 1964.

The motive power on the freight that I met as I crossed this line was not confined to tender locomotives. These trains were also seen headed by tank engines and typical were the two examples shown. The first is a 4MT Class Fairburn 2-6-4T No 42250. Regularly used for hauling goods on this line, it is seen on a down-freight on 27 August 1963. As unfitted freight trains relied solely on the brakes of the engine and guards van for stopping, they were scheduled for start to stop times giving an average of perhaps only 17 or 18 mph. Consequently, the image of the freight during the days of steam was of a train wearily plodding through the landscape. My sightings of No 42250, recorded on cine at this vantage point, show the complete opposite. It was not unusual for No 42250, given a lightish load of nine or ten wagons, to be seen travelling at 40 or 50 mph, particularly in the up direction when braking was helped by having the gradient against the train.

'It was not unusual for No 42250, given a lightish load of nine or ten wagons to be seen travelling at 40 or 50 mph ...' 4MT Class Fairburn 2-6-4T, No 42250 on down-freight - 27 August 1963.

'This class of locomotive was always intended for hauling heavy freight.' Ex-GWR 72XX Class 2-8-2T on up coal train - 24 April 1964.

Another tank engine seen regularly on these freights, was the ex-GWR 72XX Class 2-8-2T No 7207. In the view chosen, it is hauling another coal train on 24 April 1964. This class of locomotive was always intended for hauling freight. The GWR had built a series of 2-8-0Ts for working the short-haul coal trains in South Wales. The depression in the early 1930s resulted in numbers of the 2-8-0Ts being laid up. The GWR rebuilt a total of 54 2-8-0Ts into the 72XX Class of 2-8-2T, specifically for long-haul mineral freights. No 7207 was rebuilt in 1934 from 2-8-0T No 5282, which in turn had originally been built in 1930. Although 7207 was much more powerful than the Fairburn 2-6-4T, in the earlier scene there was none of the galloping style of No 42250 in the 2-8-2T as it steadily thumped along the line hauling the freight for which it had been designed.

'... joint Great Western and Great Central engine shed which presented an unhappy appearance ...' Aylesbury locomotive shed - 13 August 1966.

This pattern of traffic and locomotives was typical of the Great Western and Great Central line. There was still a good variety of Great Western locomotives, but the locomotives of the Great Central, and its successor the LNER, had been replaced and ex-LMS and BR locomotives were found instead. Today the line has been singled, and the sides of the cutting are covered in dense saplings and undergrowth, altering the picture totally.

Moving a few miles up the line to Princes Risborough, another joint Great Western and Great Central line ran up to Aylesbury. Here, at the end of the single line cross-country branch, there was a joint Great Western and Great Central engine shed which presented an unhappy appearance on 13 August 1966. Aylesbury was served by the old Great Central and Metropolitan Joint line and on the original Great Central route into London, the subject of the section that follows.

JOINT RAILS WITH THE METROPOLITAN

The Great Central Extension into London from Quainton Road in Buckinghamshire and from there until it reached Harrow South Junction, a distance of approximately 35 ½ miles, had to share the same rails as the intense Metropolitan Railways suburban services. At first it was not a successful venture because of the antipathy between the General Manager of the Great Central, Sir William Pollitt, and the Chairman and Managing Director of the Metropolitan Railway, John Bell. Such were the problems of operating their trains over this section of line that the Great Central entered into an agreement to build an alternative route bypassing the GC&Met.Jt. section entirely. Eventually, in 1901, the respective protagonists retired from their positions. Subsequent to this, an agreement was thrashed out in the following period as ratified in 1905 under the Metropolitan and Great Central Railway Act. This resulted in co-operation by both parties and the majority of the Great Central and subsequent LNER trains using the original line which was some miles shorter than the route with the Great Western.

The scenes shown on the Great Central London extension obviously reflect the motive power normally seen, day-to-day, in the period when I had changed to using colour in the camera. I am conscious that, by that date, there was little of LNER ownership from the pre-nationalisation era. Almost everywhere else I recorded pre-nationalisation built locomotives and these are reflected in those pictures chosen. Should the Great Central line enthusiasts have opened this book at the back, then I can only refer them to the Introduction where, in an effort to restore the balance, I have included some black and white scenes from Neasden shed in pre-nationalisation days.

The joint line ran, and still does run, through Great Missenden, some 9 miles south of Aylesbury and 29 miles from Marylebone. For two or three years, my journeys took me through Great Missenden in the evenings on the way home. In the summer, I would occasionally see the smoke and steam of a waiting train. If the day had not been too tiring, I would sometimes turn round and go and have a look. It was always the same train, an up-stopping parcels, which reversed into a siding in order that a DMU service to Marylebone could pass. The siding was well suited to photography being on a low embankment and the light coming from the best direction.

'The number 1337 and shed, never actually carried by the locomotive, have been carefully chalked on the buffer beam in the LNER style.'
B1 Class 4-6-0, BR No 61337 at Great Missenden. This locomotive, and all others in this section, are on an up-stopping parcels waiting for the road after being passed by an up local DMU - 9 July 1963.

As the previous section did not show any LNER locomotives on the joint line, I have started with two shots which partly redresses that omission. These show B1 Class 4-6-0, No 61337 on 9 July 1963. While this locomotive is an LNER design, it was actually a BR locomotive built by the North British Locomotive Co, after nationalisation. According to the RCTS *Locomotives of the LNER* (The Railway Correspondence and Travel Society, 1975), this engine was one of the longest surviving B1 Class locomotives, withdrawn in company with 61030 and 61306, in September 1967. Even after 15 years of nationalisation, railwaymen's old loyalties died hard. The number 1337 and shed, never actually carried by the locomotive, have been carefully chalked on the buffer beam in the LNER style. The train itself would have a formation which varied from day to day. The B1 was hardly tested in hauling two full brakes and two vans, the entire train would have been less than 100 tons.

Exactly a week after the B1 was recorded on the parcels on 16 July 1963, I found Class 5, 4-6-0, No 44830 doing this turn of duty. For a run-of-the-mill Class 5 locomotive, it was in a respectable condition as these were not normally clean enough for the lining to show. The opportunity has been taken in this shot, and in the next, to comment further on the movable top feed to this class of locomotive. The top feed would introduce water into the boiler onto a tray which spread the cold water over as large an area as practical, before it came into contact with the boiling water already in the boiler. With standardisation supposed to be the name of the game, it would be reasonable to assume that there was a standard position for the top feed. Not so, and I am one enthusiast who has never understood why such a fundamental part of the boiler should become a variable fixture. On No 44830 the top feed can be seen at the furthest position back along the boiler.

'... this engine was one of the longest surviving B1 Class locomotives ...'
B1 Class 4-6-0, BR No 61337 at Great Missenden - 9 July 1963.

'For a run-of-the-mill Class 5
locomotive, it was in a
respectable condition ...'
Class 5, 4-6-0, BR No 44830 at
Great Missenden - 16 July 1963.

'... and the steam under the cab is probably indicative of the fireman having problems in getting the injectors to work ...'
Class 5, 4-6-0, BR No 45334 at Great Missenden - 26 July 1963.

'... something depressing about an engine in service which had lost its name plate before withdrawal.'
Ex-LMS Royal Scot Class 4-6-0, BR No 46163 *Civil Service Rifleman* at Great Missenden - 21 April 1964.

Turn to the next scene, and I have included a shot of another ex-LMS example of the Class 5 , 4-6-0, BR No 45334. This was photographed on 26 July 1963 and it can be seen to be much dirtier than No 44830 and probably that much longer out of the shops. On 45334 the top feed is right forward on the boiler and the steam under the cab is probably indicative of the fireman having problems in getting the injectors to work, necessary to get water into the boiler. The steam at the front of the engine will have come from the cylinders. The cylinder cocks would have been left open while standing for two reasons. First, if there was a leak in the regulator while the engine was standing, it could lead to a build-up in the cylinders and the engine could move off on its own. Second, while standing, the steam would condense in the cylinders. When the engine next started, the water in the cylinders could force the end of the cylinders off and even bend the connecting rods. Leaving the cylinder cocks open avoided this by forcing any water out of the cylinders. Good operating practice dictated that the cylinder cocks were opened when the engine stopped.

The last photograph in this section is of an ex-LMS Royal Scot Class 4-6-0, BR No 46163 *Civil Service Rifleman*. This is in a much better condition than its sister engine No 46156 shown earlier in the section on Woodford shed. However, like No 46156 at Woodford, No 46163 here also had its name plate removed. There was something depressing about an engine in service which had lost its name plate before withdrawal. Clearly there were some employees who felt the same way because on the Isle of Wight a number of locomotives were given painted wooden replica name boards after the original plate had been removed. Somehow that action restored an engine's dignity.

Finale

FINALE

To close the book on the downbeat note set by my picture and comments of the Royal Scot in the last section could give a totally unwarranted view of how I look back at that period. I felt that I should close with the sight of locomotives that gave great pleasure just to see.

The choice fell on two such locomotives, both seen on the same day. The date was 13 August 1966, when 'The Railway Correspondence and Travel Society' ran a 'special' over Great Central rails. The event had a very ambitious itinerary. Starting from Waterloo, it worked its way round west London to join the old Great Central line from the Midland goods line at Neasden. From there the tour was all Great Central or Great Central joint lines. The direct route through Aylesbury, using the GC&Met joint route, was taken to Nottingham Victoria. This was followed by a tour of Great Central lines as far as Penistone on the original Manchester and Sheffield route. From there, the run was down to Sheffield (Victoria), Nottingham (Victoria) for a second time, and a run to Marylebone via Princes Risborough and the Great Central & Great Western joint line.

Curious are the highlights that memory recalls of such a journey. The special had lost considerable time due to the need for the refreshment car requiring its water tanks to be refilled. Consequently, the journey south from about Leicester onwards was in the dark. In order for the train to take the line across to the Great Western, the signal box at Grendon Underwood Junction, just south of Calvert, had to remain open. The layout of the junction was in favour of trains taking the direct route, and the special observed the slack religiously, probably not exceeding 20 or 25 mph. As we slowly ran past the signal box, it was possible to see from the light in the box, the signalman watching our train pass. What has stuck in my memory was that in 1966, the signal box at such a junction was still only lit by an oil lamp.

Enough of the irrelevant memories - now to return to the record of two of the locomotives that were in charge that day. The first is of an ex-Southern Railway, unrebuilt West Country Class 4-6-2, BR No 34002 *Salisbury* shown waiting to leave Waterloo with the special. This engine was only the second locomotive of the West Country Class Pacifics to be built, entering service in June 1945. It is difficult to appreciate that this engine,

'... the second locomotive of the West Country Class Pacifics to be built, entering service in June 1945.' Ex-Southern Railway, unrebuilt West Country Class Pacific 4-6-2, BR No 34002 *Salisbury* at Waterloo station - 13 August 1966.

'... Nottingham (Victoria), a station seemingly carved out of solid rock, in the centre of the city.' Ex-LMS Stanier 8F 2-8-0, BR No 48197, backing down onto RCTS special at Nottingham (Victoria) - 13 August 1966.

turned out in such a superb exterior condition, would be withdrawn by British Rail only eight months later.

Salisbury ran the train from Waterloo to Nottingham (Victoria), a station seemingly carved out of solid rock, in the centre of the city. At Nottingham, the West Country was replaced by an ex-LMS 8F 2-8-0, BR No 48197. A Robinson Great Central 2-8-0 would have been more appropriate for the run over the old Great Central freight lines that were to follow. However, I believe I am correct in saying that, by August 1966, the last remaining examples of Robinson's 2-8-0 design had been withdrawn earlier in the year. The choice of the LMS 8F was most acceptable in the circumstances.

Seen here is No 48197 backing down onto the train. Again, the locomotive has been turned out in a condition that more than complements the presentation of *Salisbury* when taking over at the head of the train. Even the coal in the tender seems to have been specially selected. It is also pleasant to be able to close on a well turned-out 8F 2-8-0 after the less-than-pristine condition of those shown elsewhere in this book, while slogging it out on freight after freight. Somehow this view restores the balance and shows that the Stanier 2-8-0 really was an engine that could catch the eye.

INDEX TO ILLUSTRATIONS OF LOCOMOTIVES

This index has been compiled with reference only to those illustrations showing locomotives. It has been adjudged that those most likely to refer to the index require a pictorial reference of a certain class of locomotive or even a particular locomotive. Each reference will be found under the heading showing ownership of the locomotive at the date of the photograph with the exception of Industrial locomotives which are grouped under their respective builders. Individual references identify the locomotive by its number, name, wheel arrangement and type.